ILLUSIONS

Daniele Serra

ILLUSIONS

A Black Coat Press Book

Dedicated to Mara

A huge thanks to:
Roy K. Robbins (Bad Moon Books), J.-M. Lofficier (Black Coat Press), Larry Roberts (Bloodletting Press), Michael Bernoudy (Bluphier), Dawn Rivers Baker (Brighid's Fire Books), Mindy Jarusek (Cemetery Dance), James Williamson (Creation Oneiros), Joe Morey (Dark Regions Press), Pam Marin-Kingsley (Darkhart Press), Kwanza Johnson and Ron Perazza (DC Comics), Eric Enk, Giacomo Pisano, J. Travis Grundon, James Havoc, Jessica Redmerski, John Grover, Joseph Mcgee, Lisa Mannetti, Adrian Kaheaku (Leucrota Press), David Montoya (Magus Press), Matt Venne, Michael Louis Calvillo, James Curcio and P. Emerson Williams (Mythos Media), Nick Doan, Nick Valentino, Rain Graves, R.W. Wells, Shaun Jeffrey, Adam Huber (Snuff Books), Steven Savile, Jeff Mariotte, Tara Vanflower, Steve Clark (Tasmaniac Press), Stephen H. Segal (*Weird Tales* magazine), Liz Burton (Zumaya Publications).

Contact:
daniele@multigrade.it
Visit the artist's website:
http://www.multigrade.it/
Visit our website at www.blackcoatpress.com

ISBN 978-1-934543-87-0. First Printing May 2009. Published by Black Coat Press, an imprint of Hollywood Comics.com, LLC, P.O. Box 17270, Encino, CA 91416. All rights reserved. Except for review purposes, no part of this book may be reproduced or transmitted in any form or by any means, electronic or mechanical, including photocopying, recording, or by any information storage and retrieval system, without permission in writing from the artist or the publisher. Printed in the United States of America.

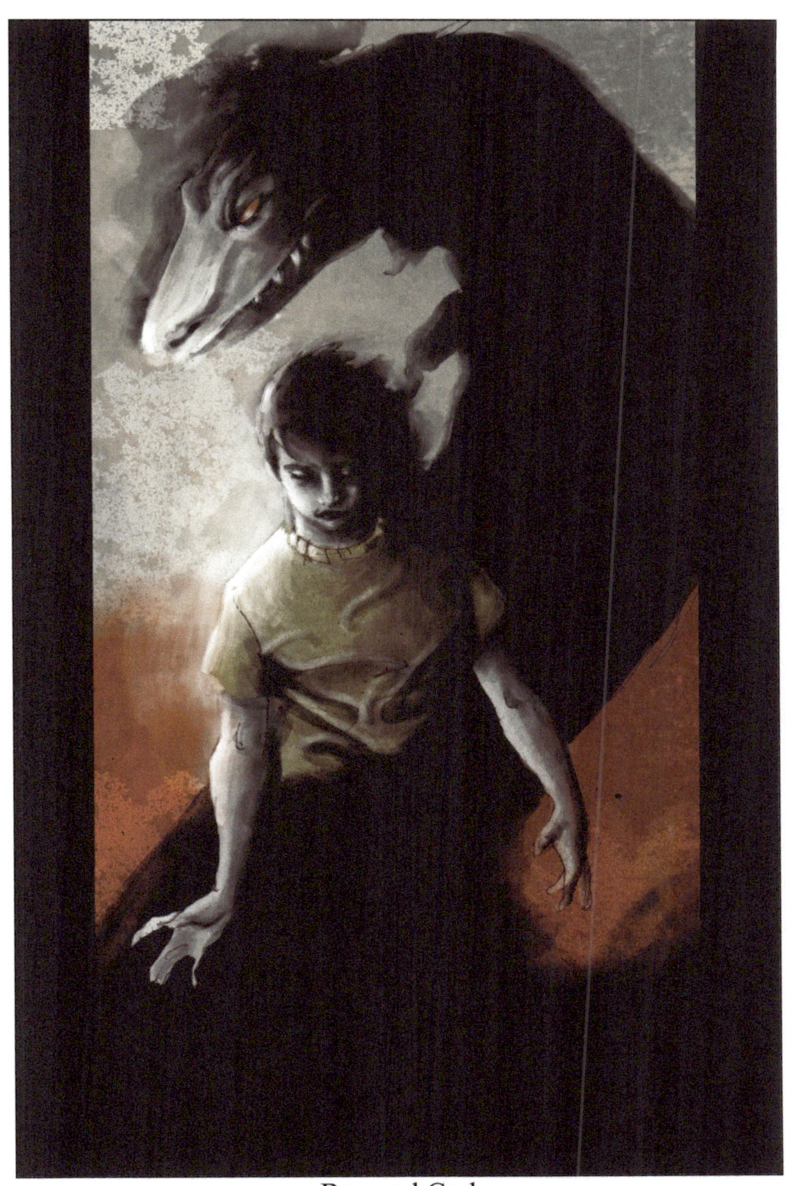

Boy and God

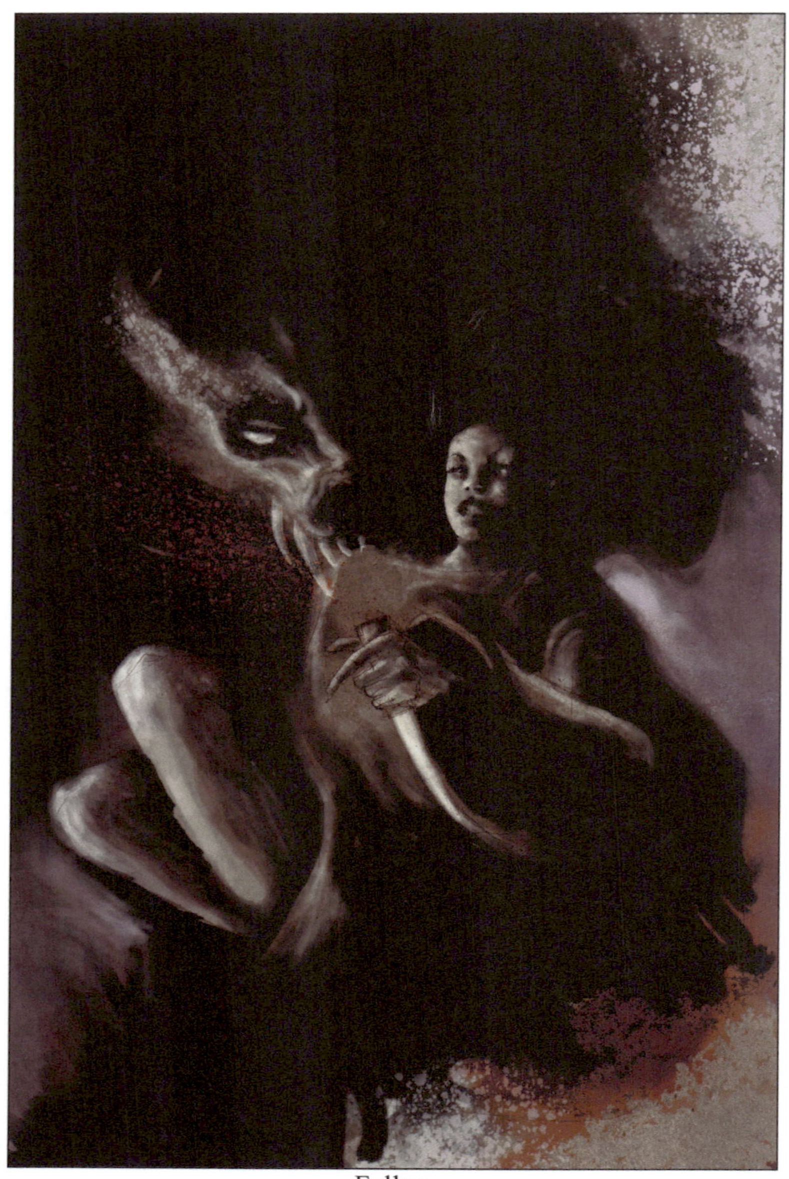

Fallon

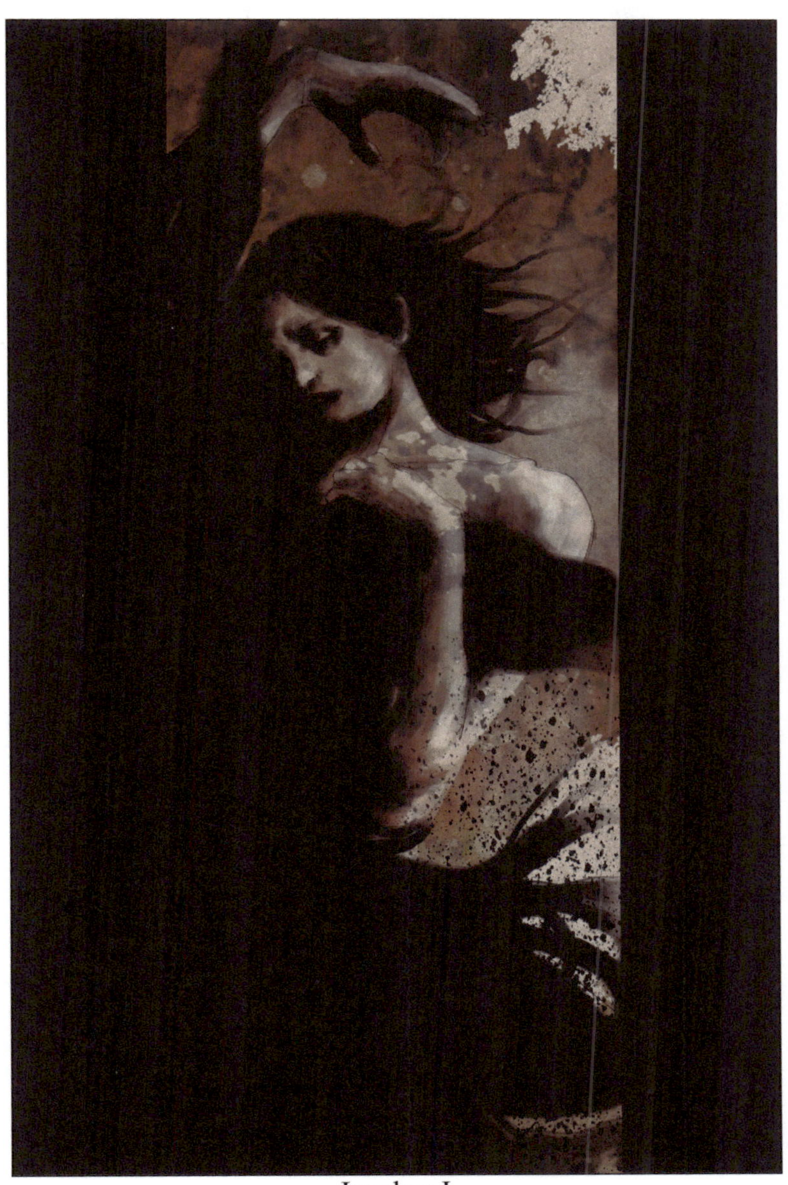

Incubus I

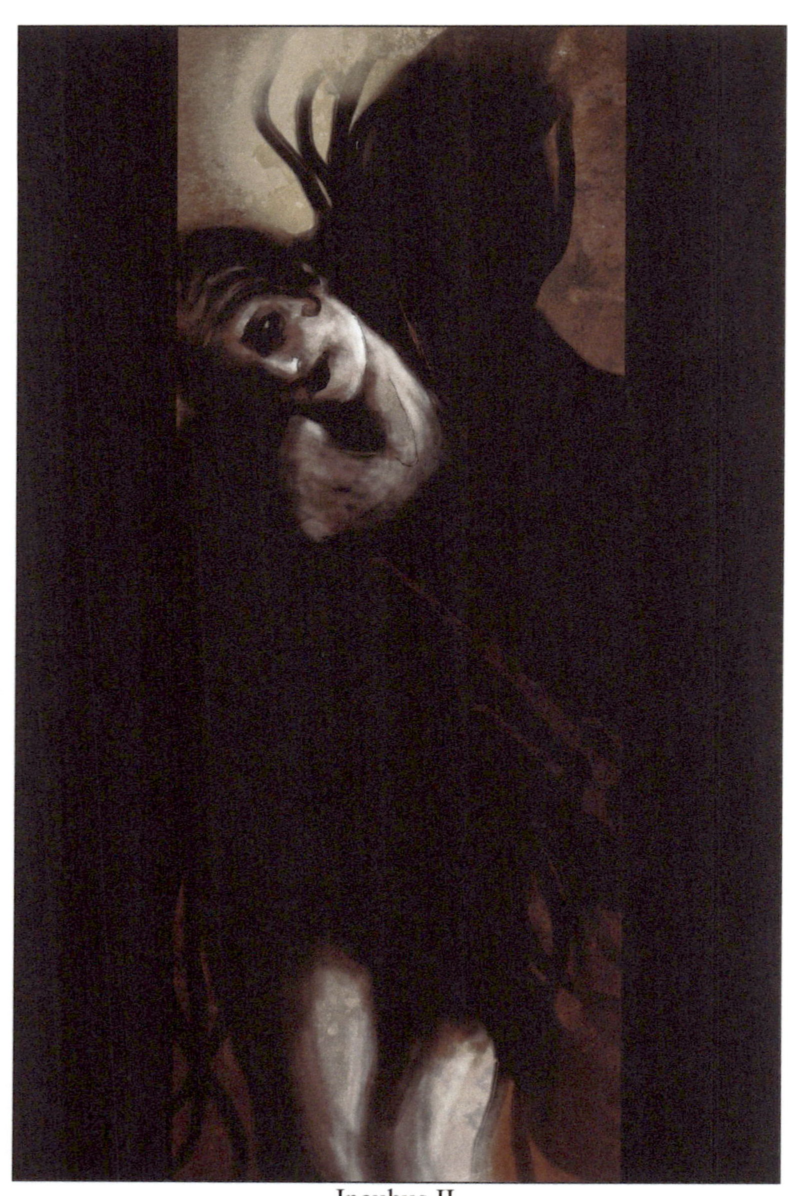

Incubus II

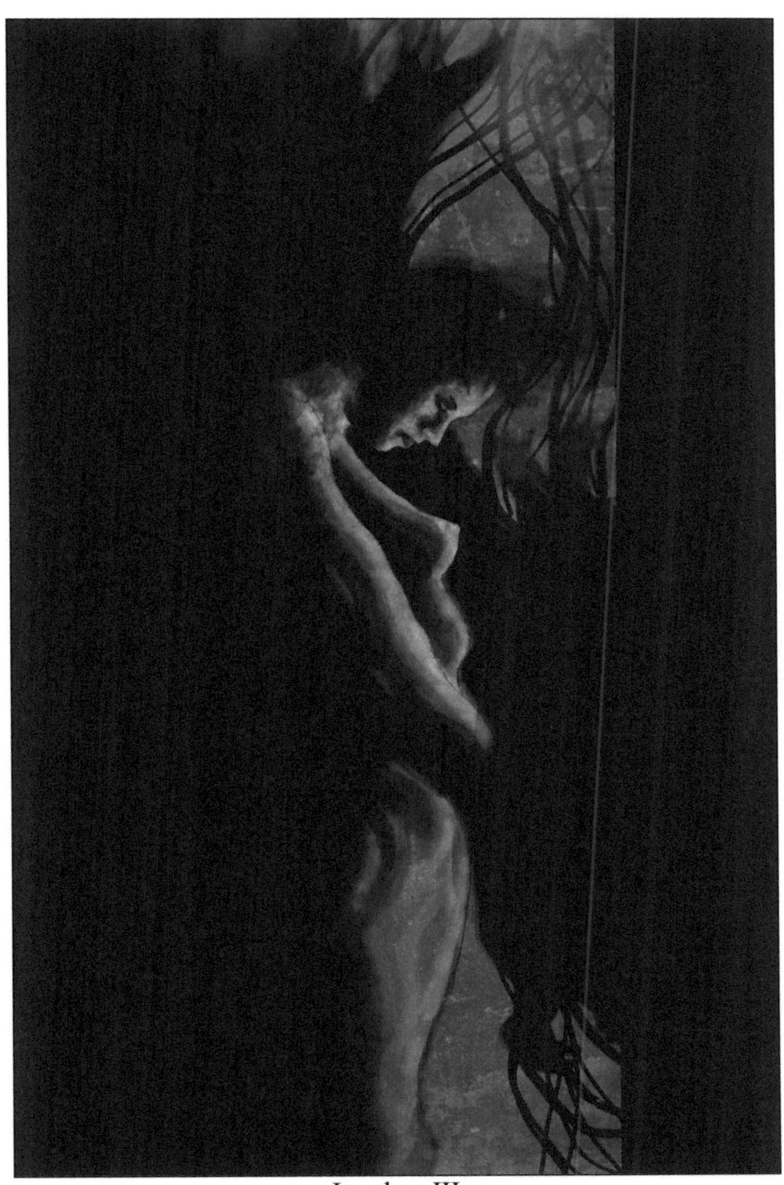

Incubus III

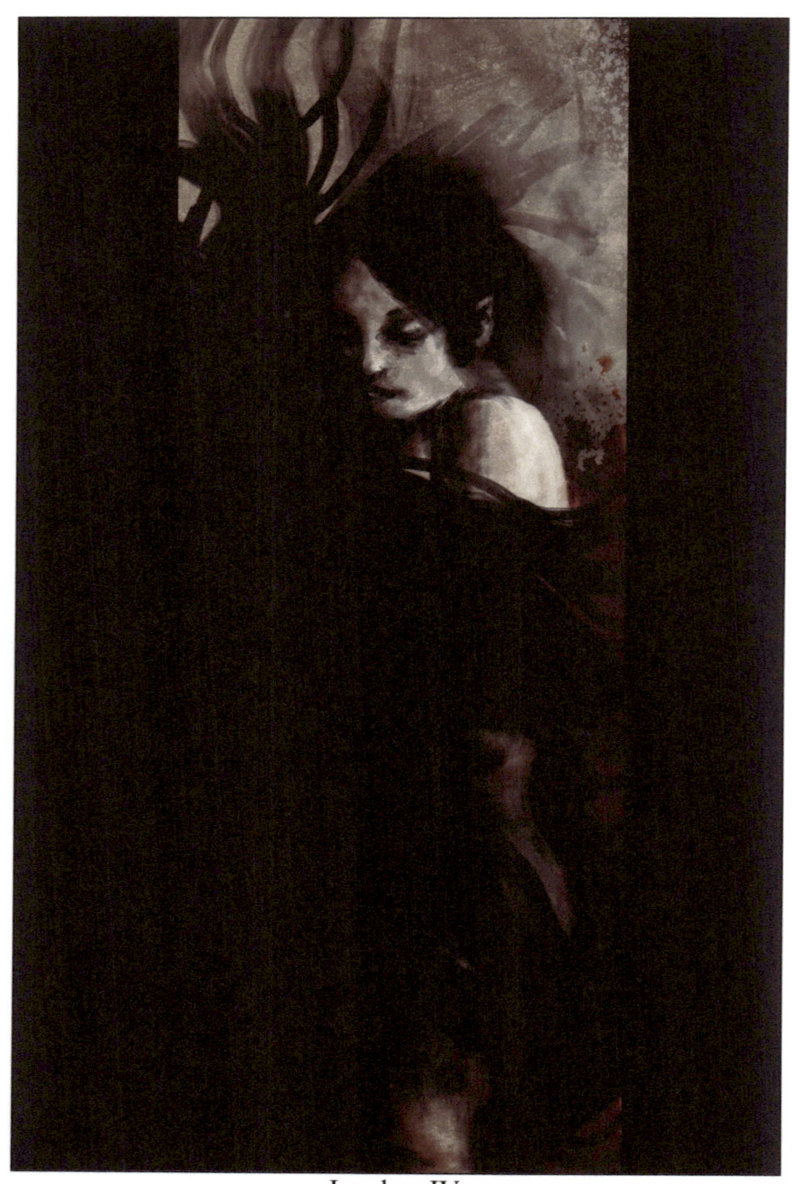

Incubus IV

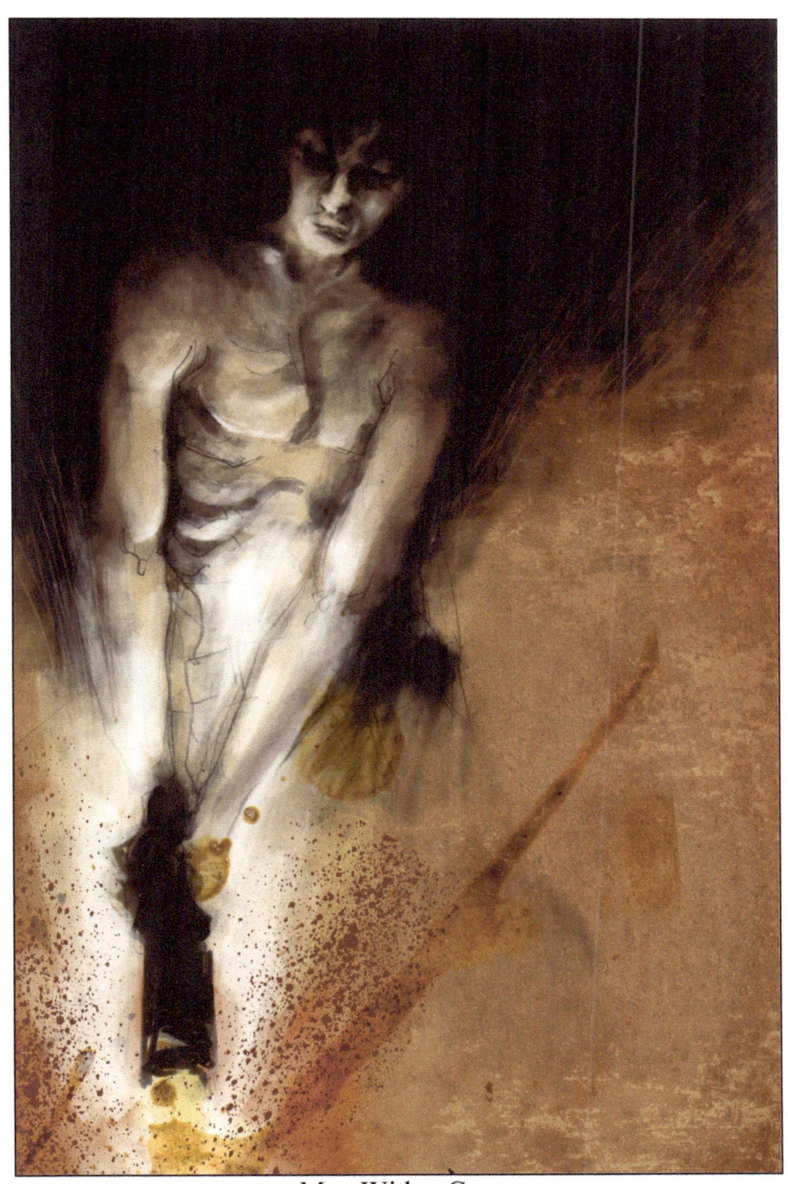

Man With a Gun

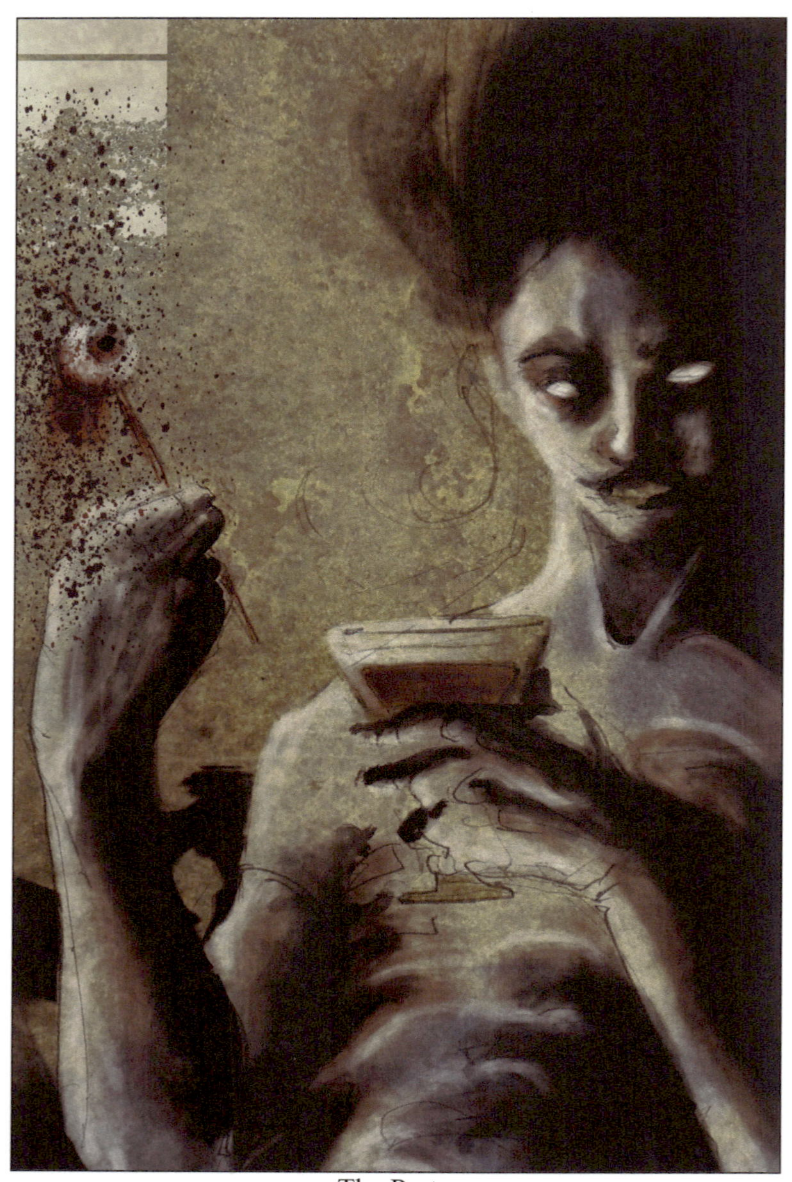

The Party

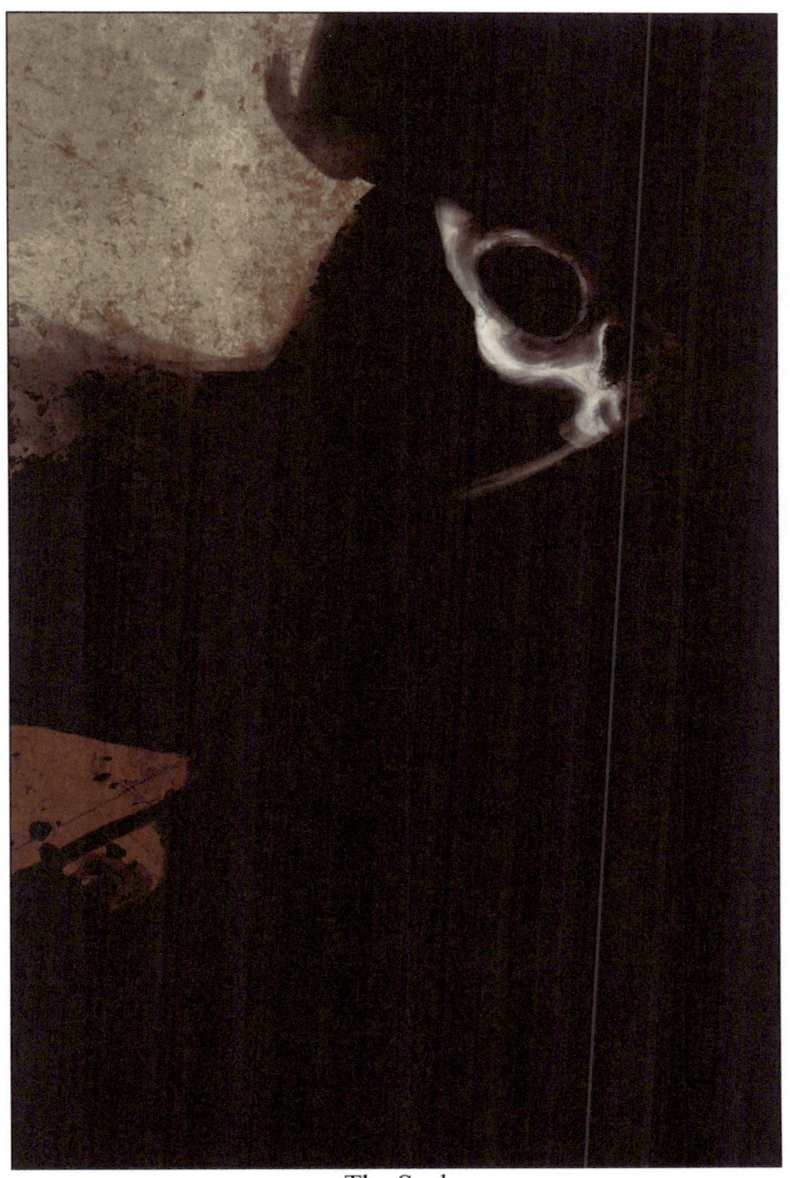

The Seal

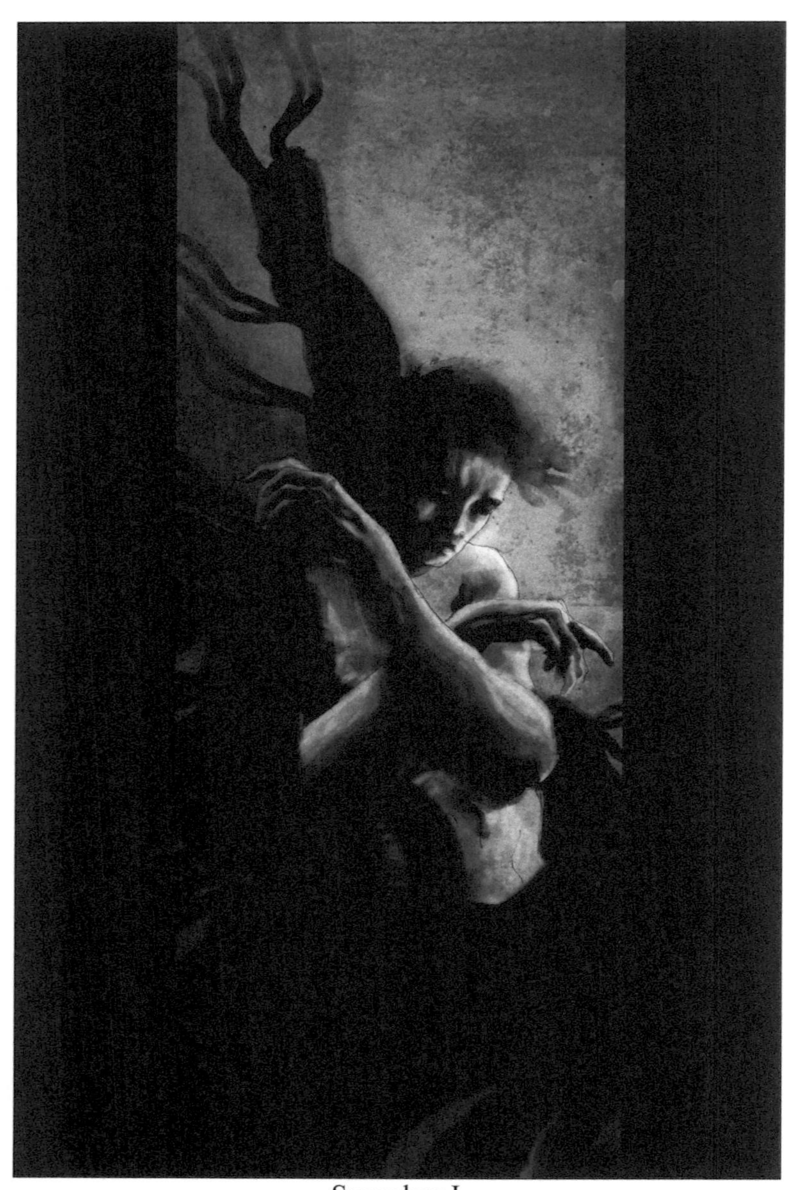

Succubus I

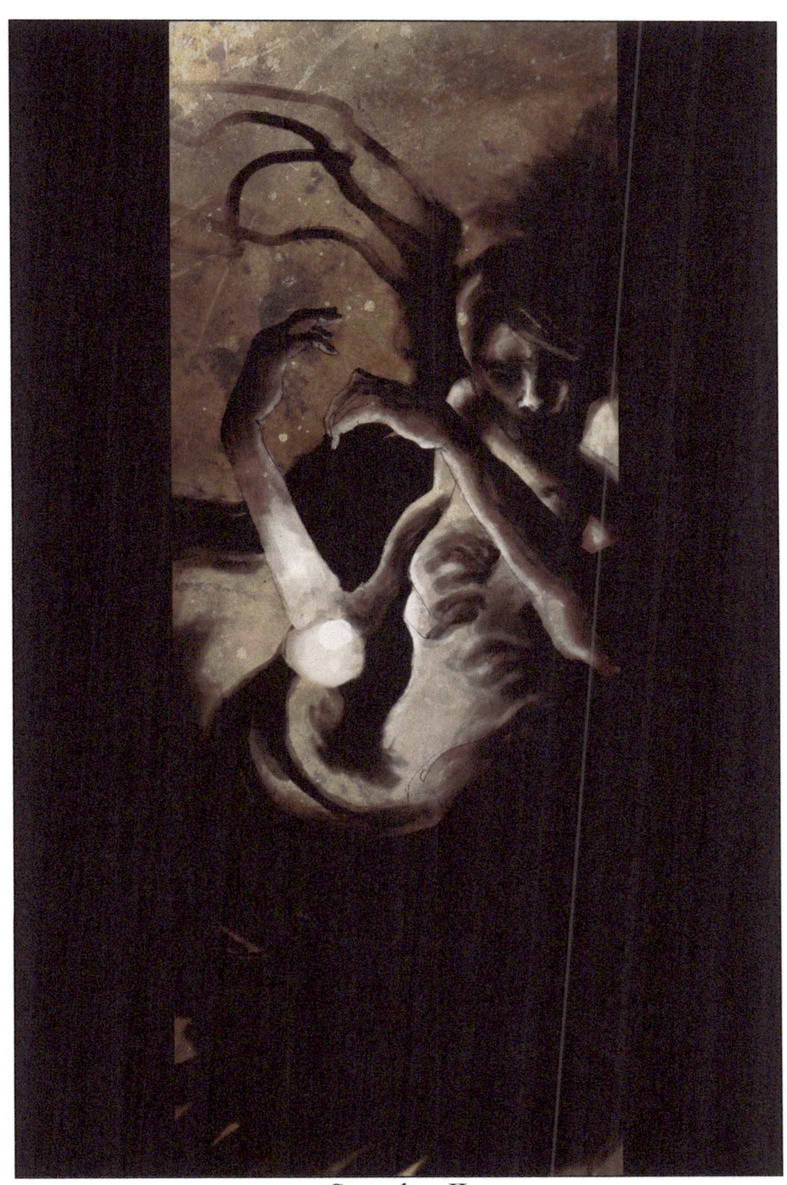

Succubus II

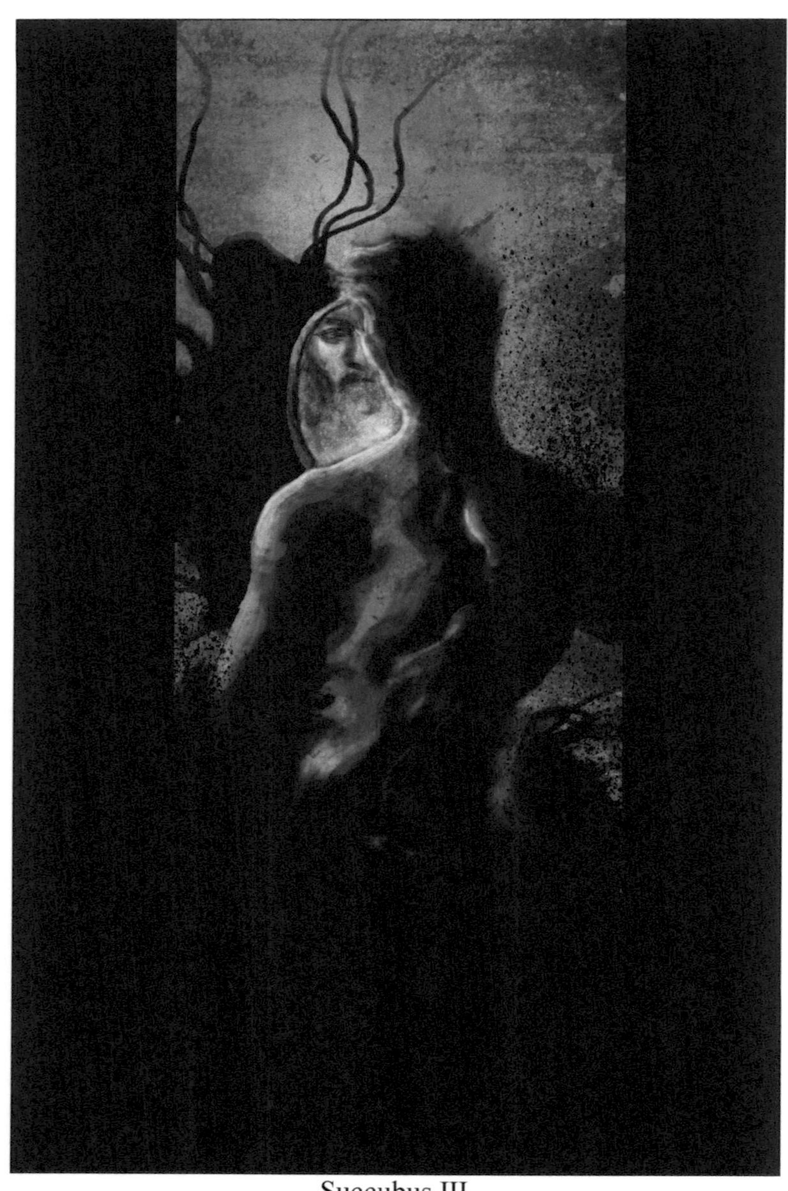

Succubus III

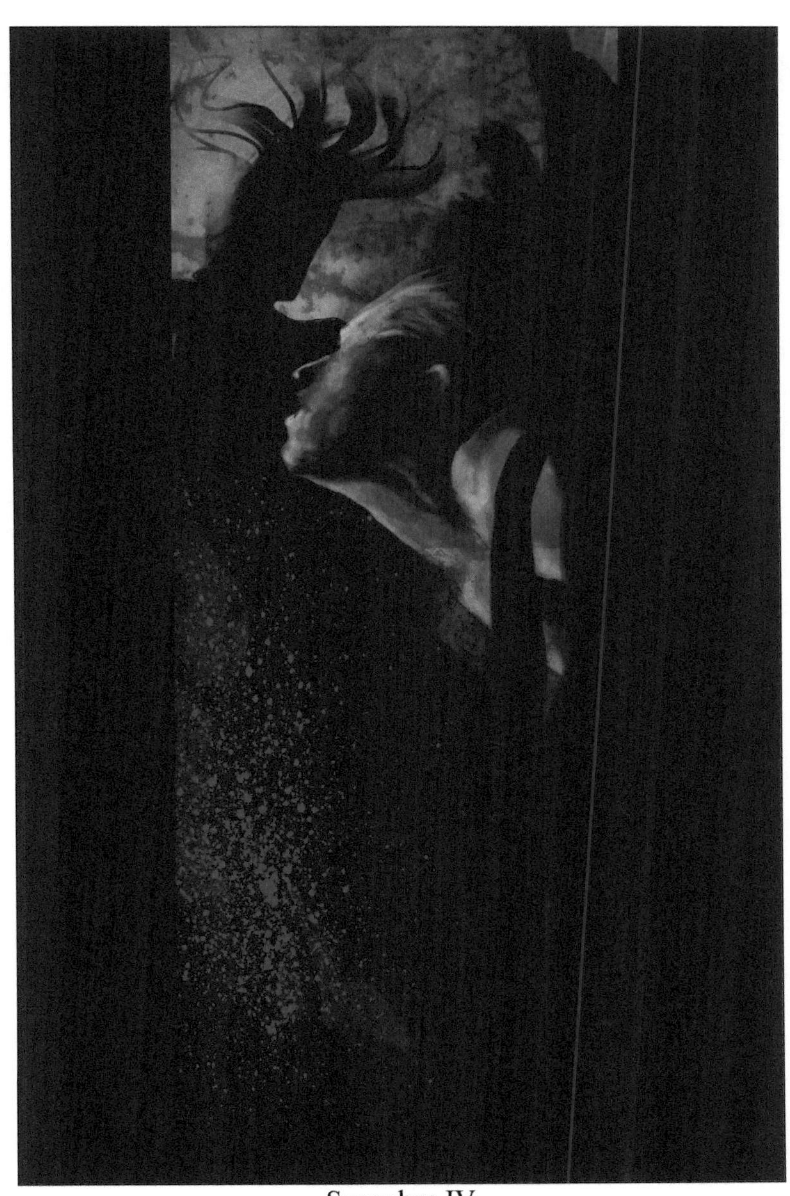

Succubus IV

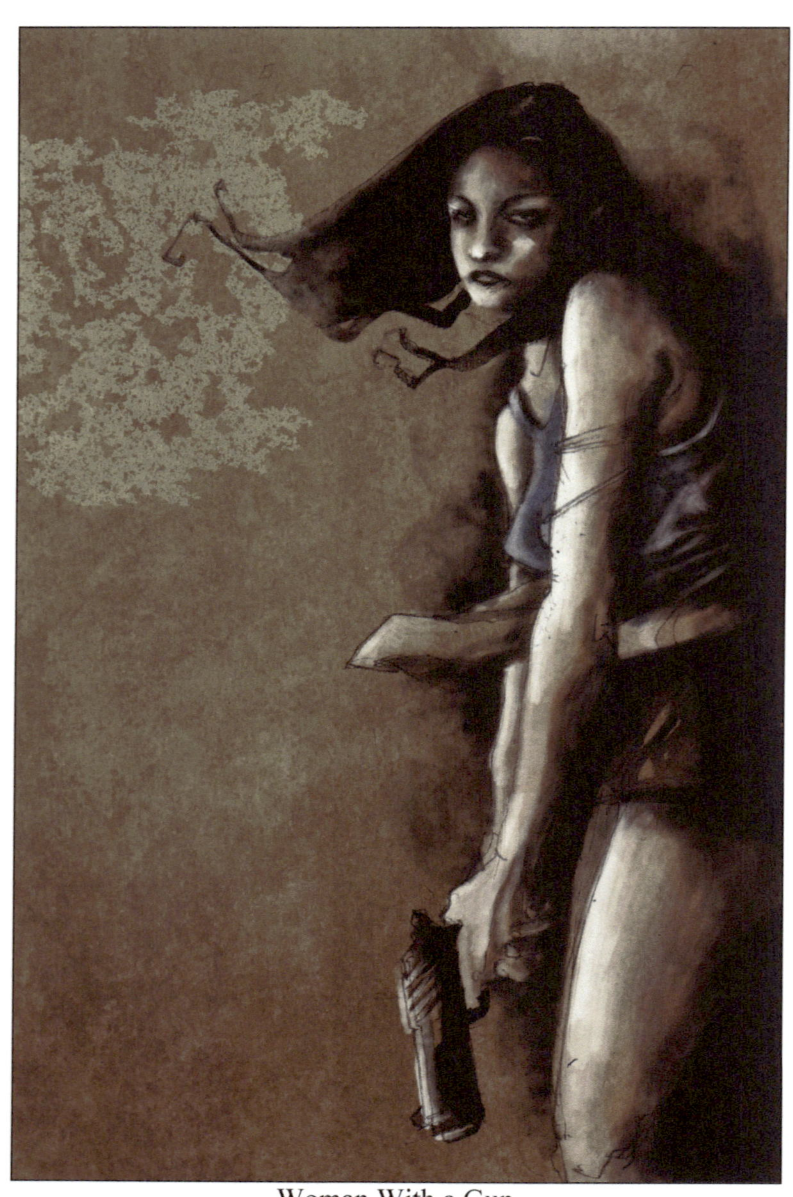

Woman With a Gun

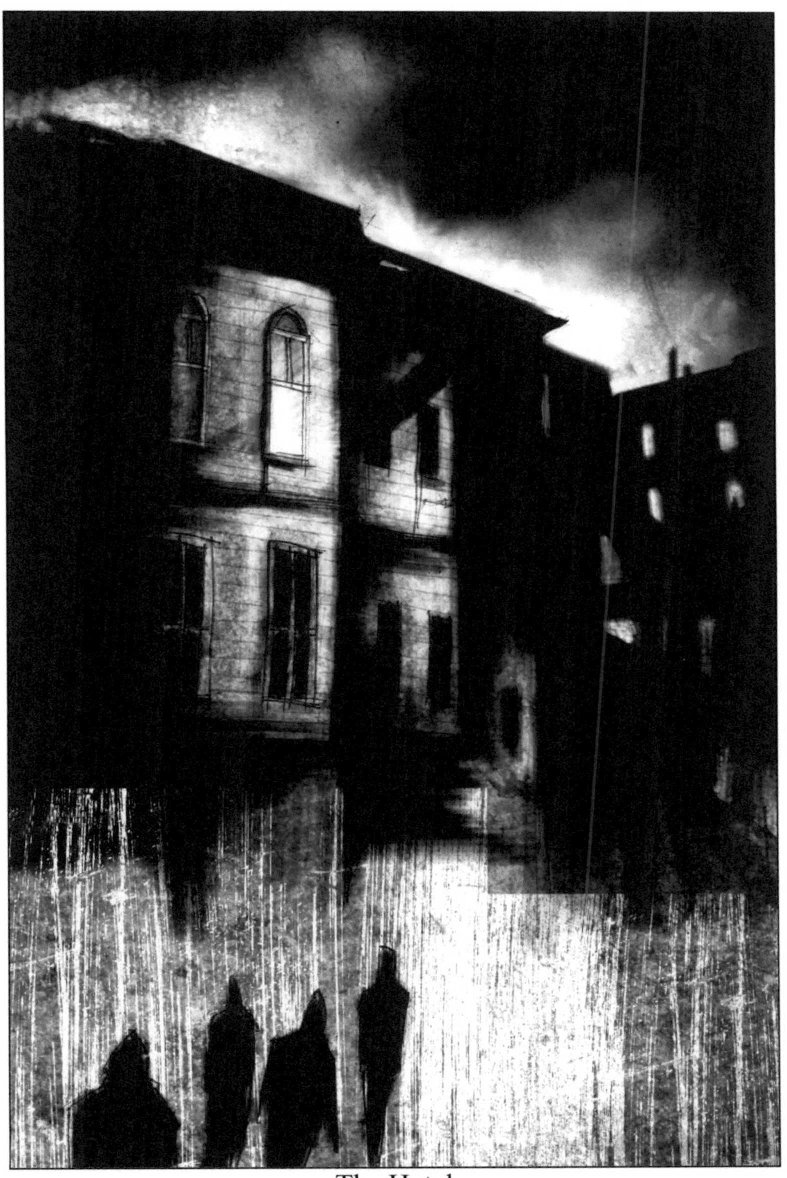

The Hotel

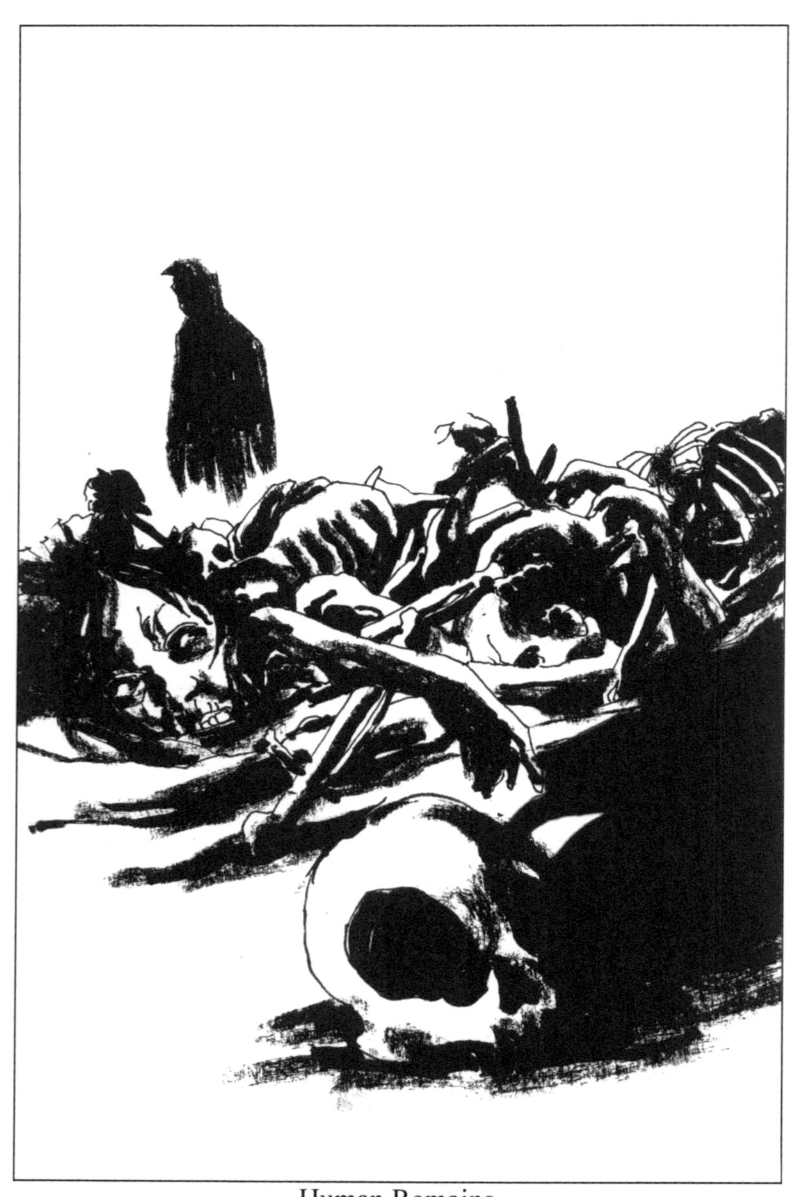

Human Remains

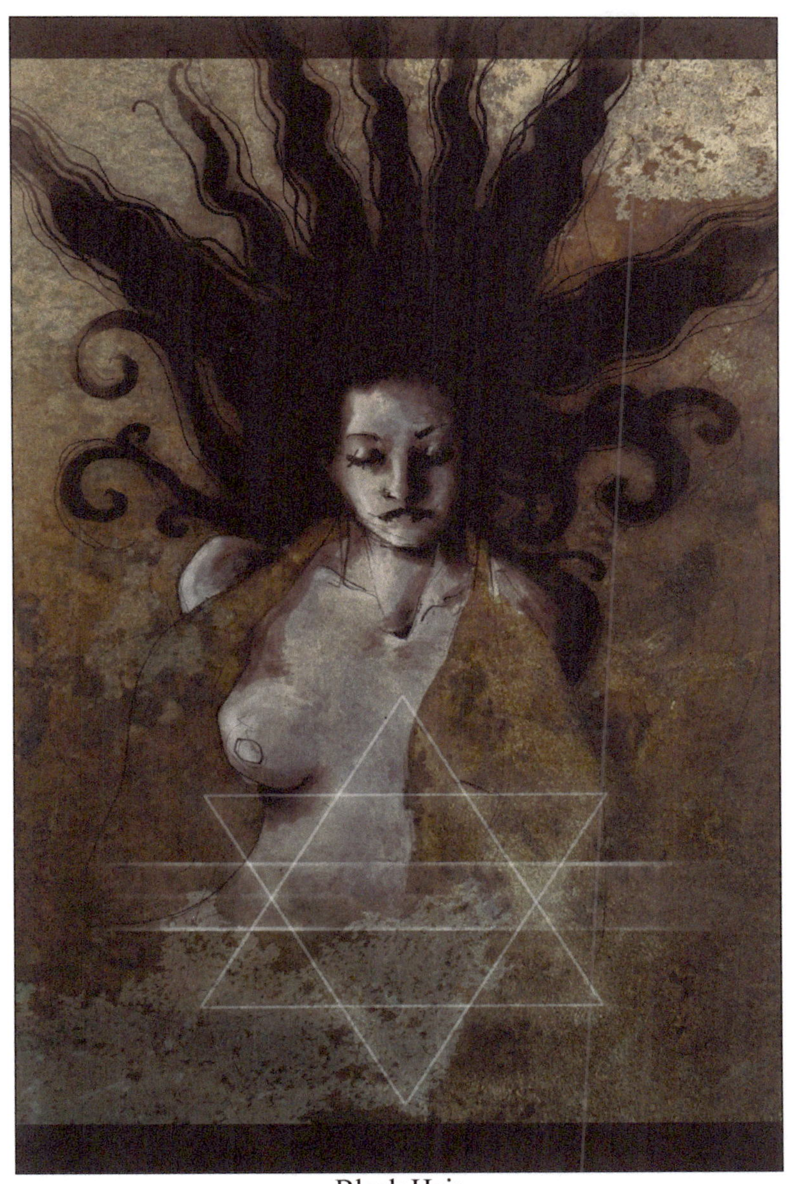

Black Hair

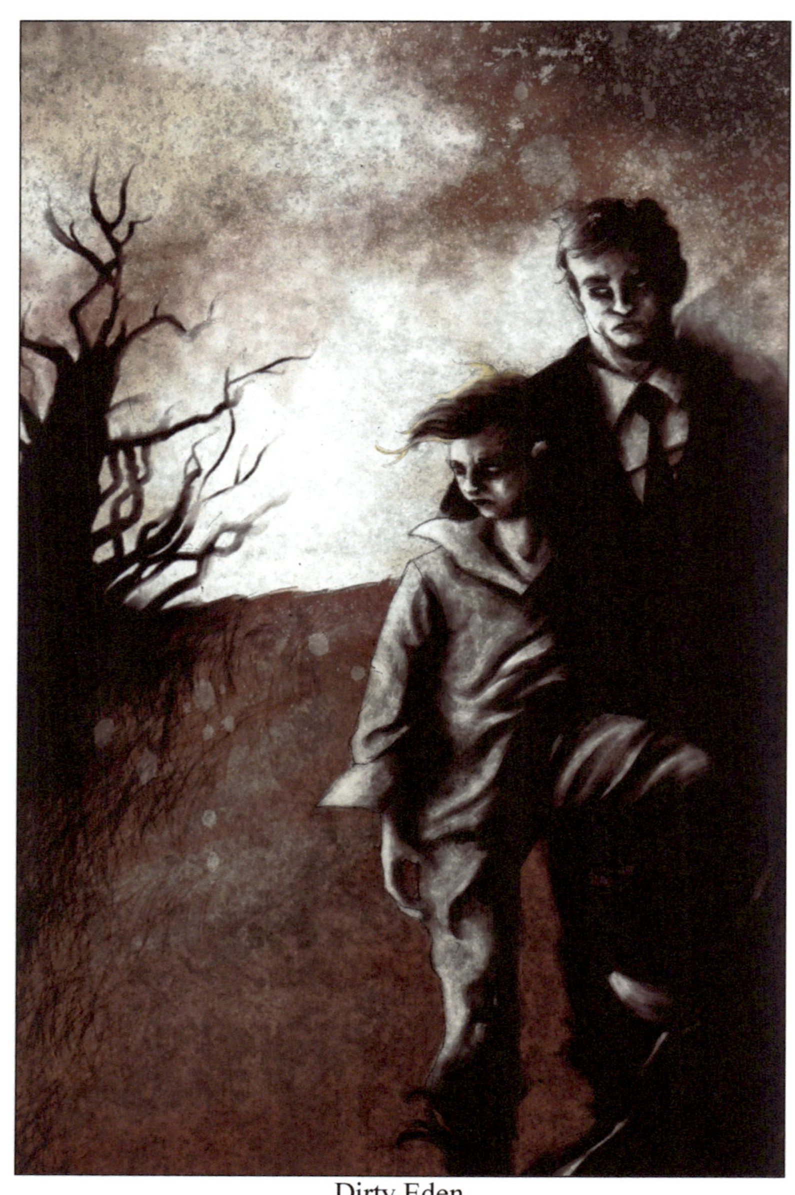

Dirty Eden

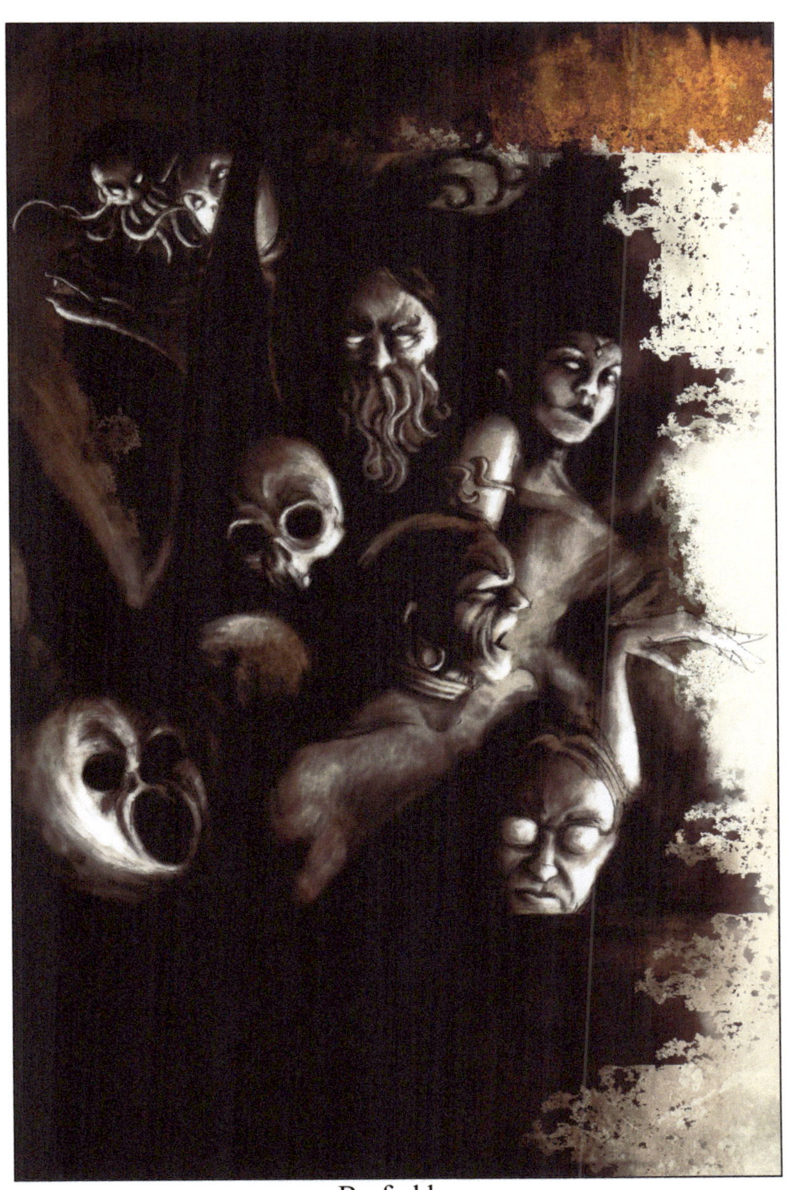

Barfodder

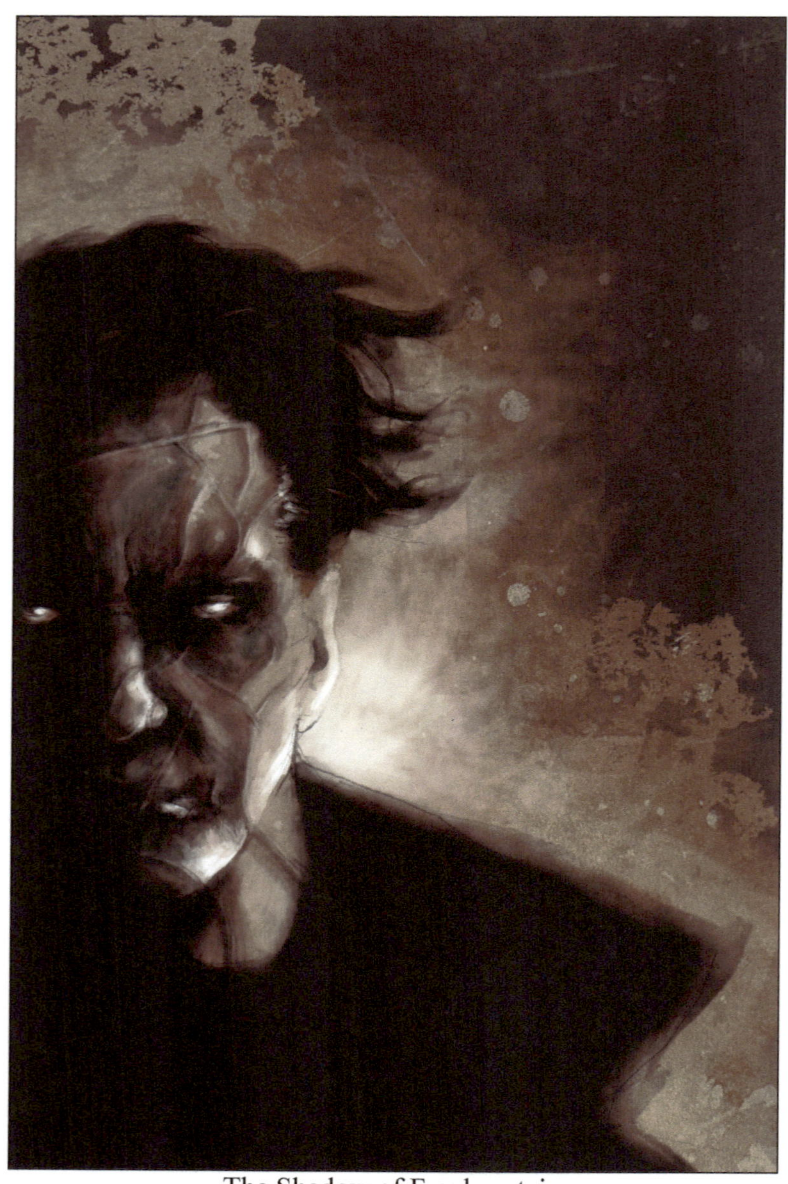

The Shadow of Frankenstein

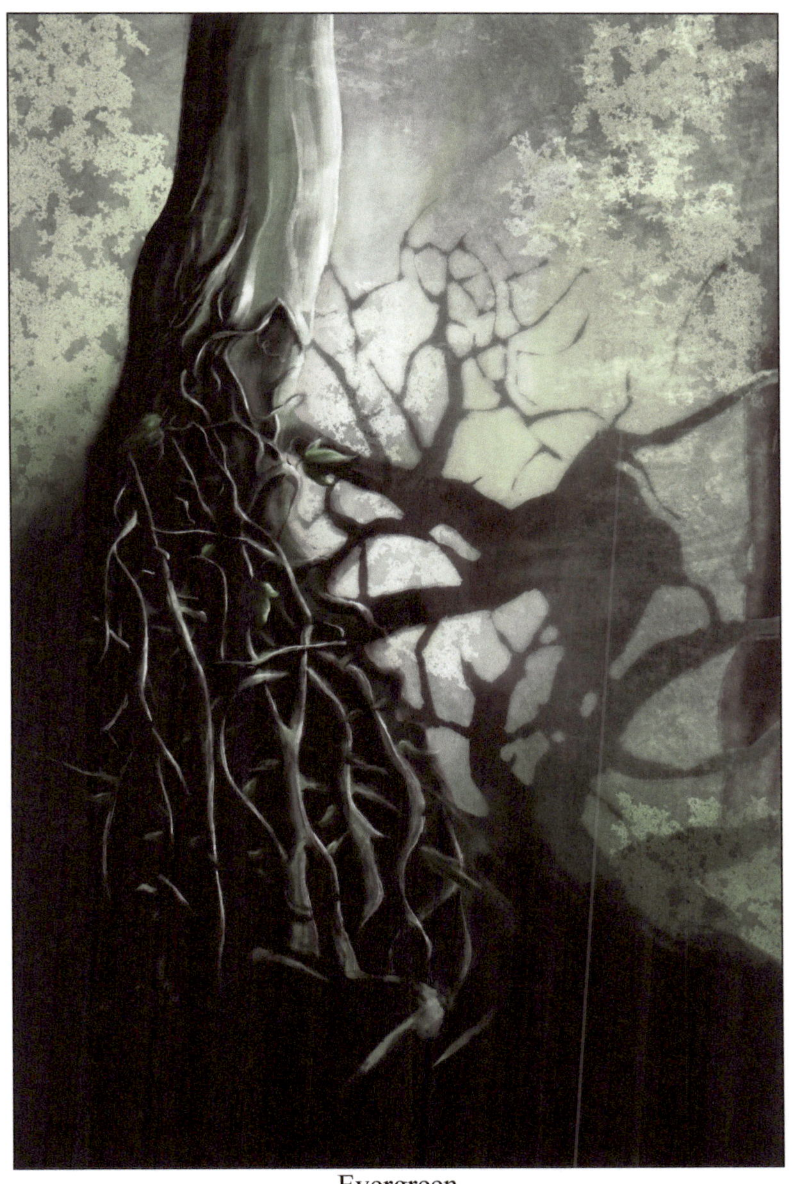

Evergreen

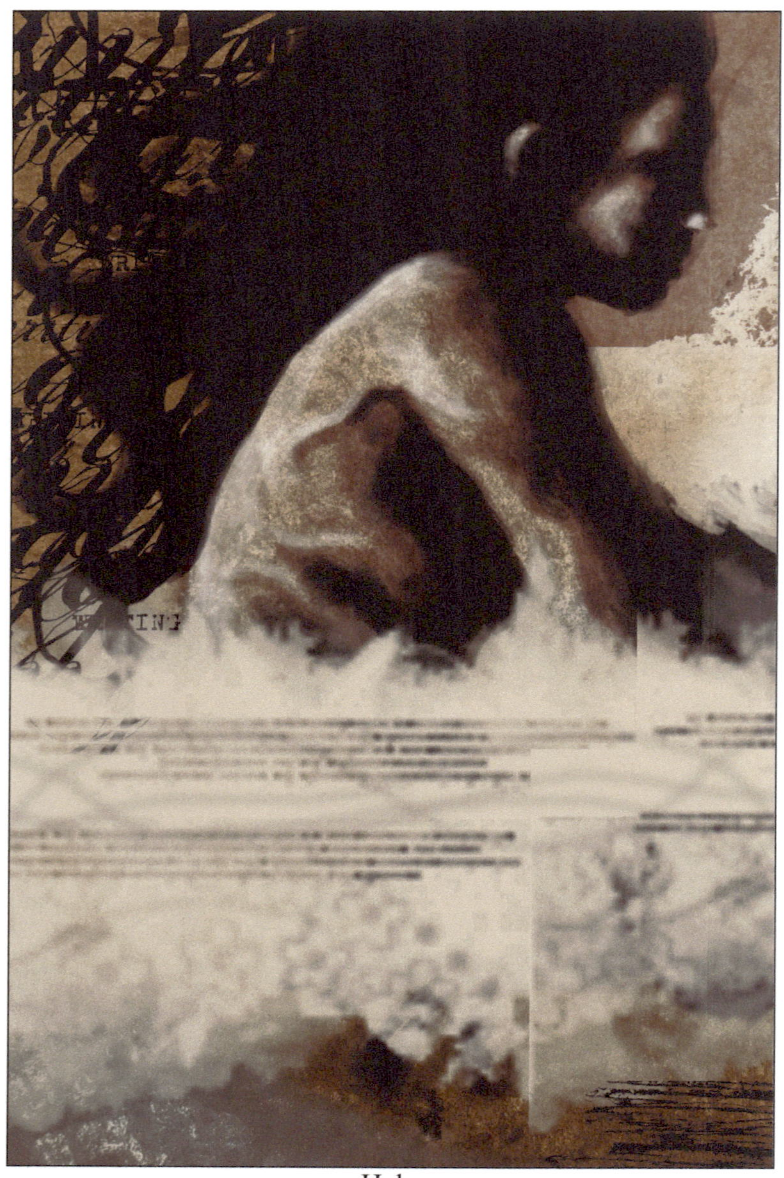

Help

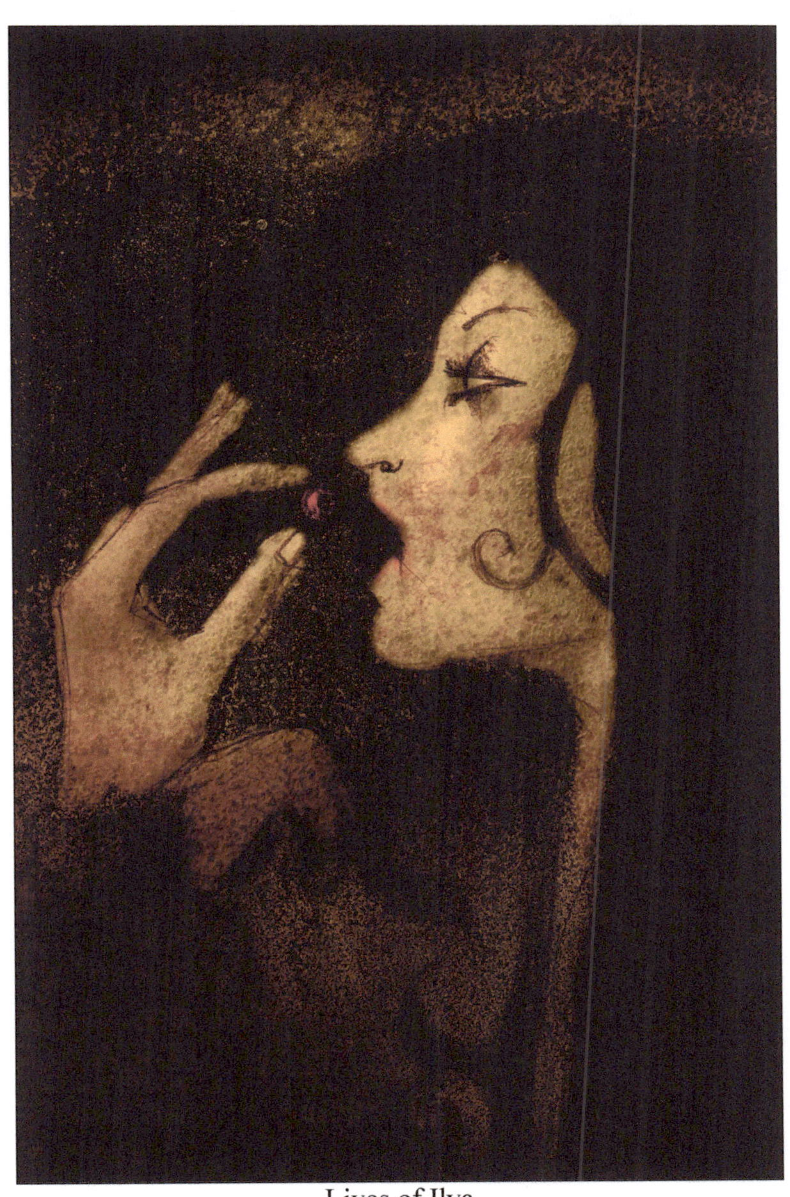

Lives of Ilya

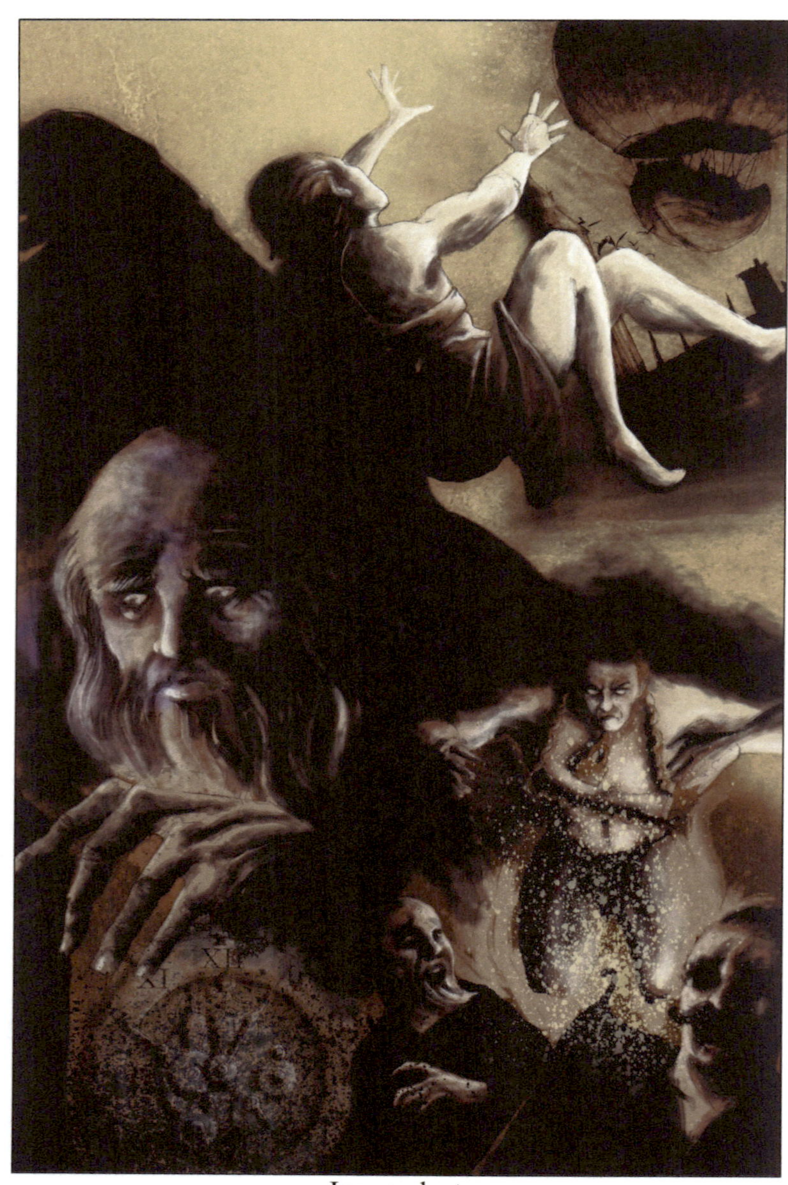

Incompleat

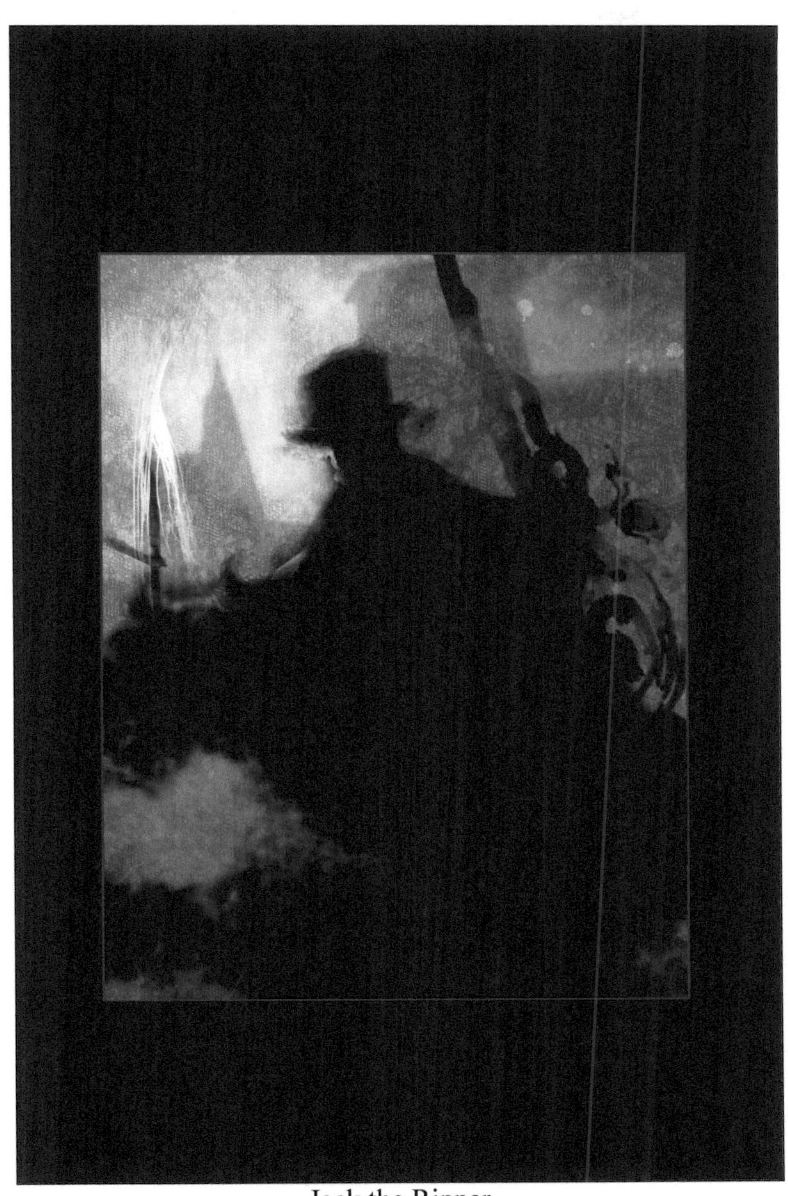

Jack the Ripper

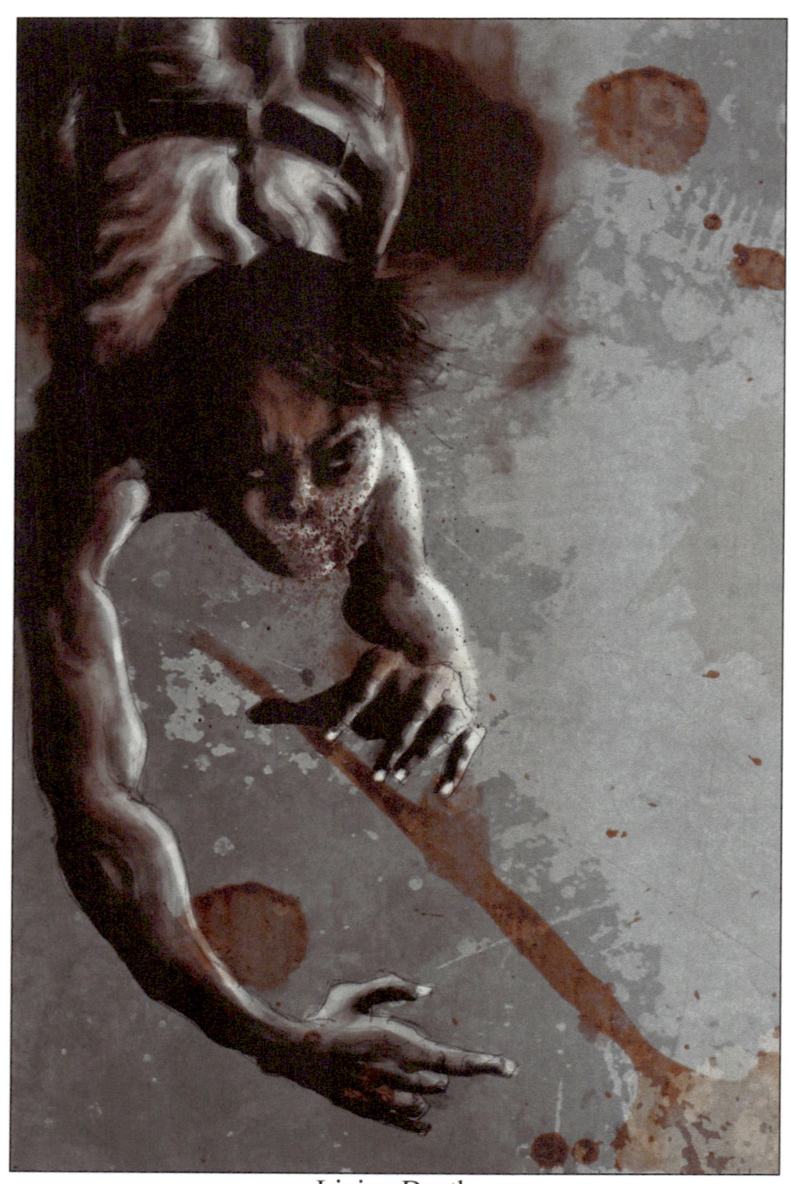

Living Death

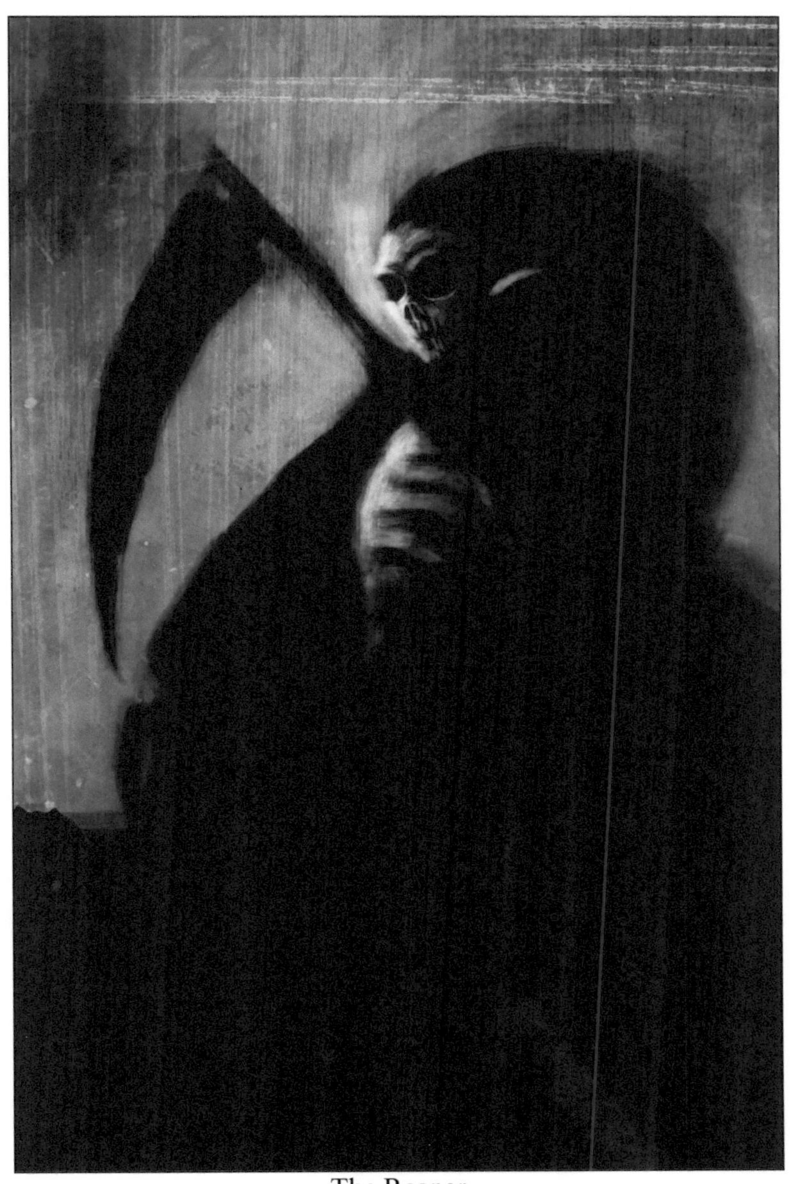

The Reaper

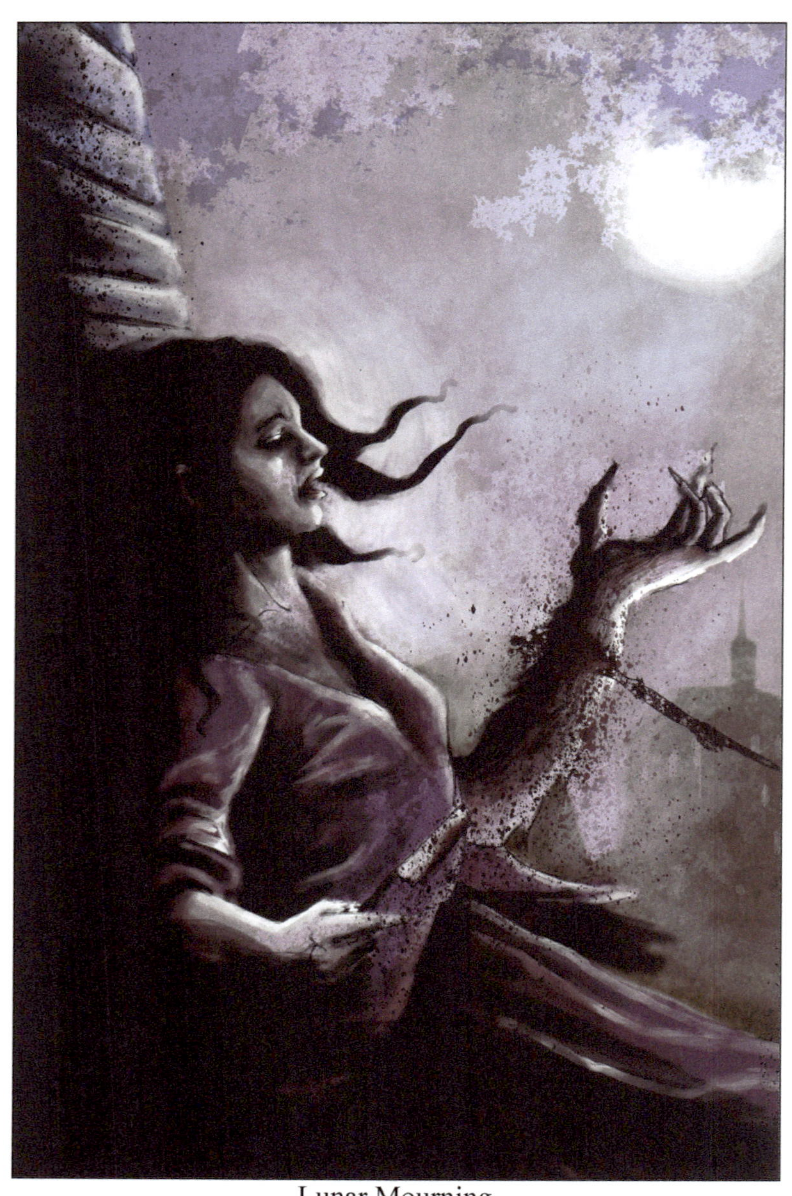

Lunar Mourning

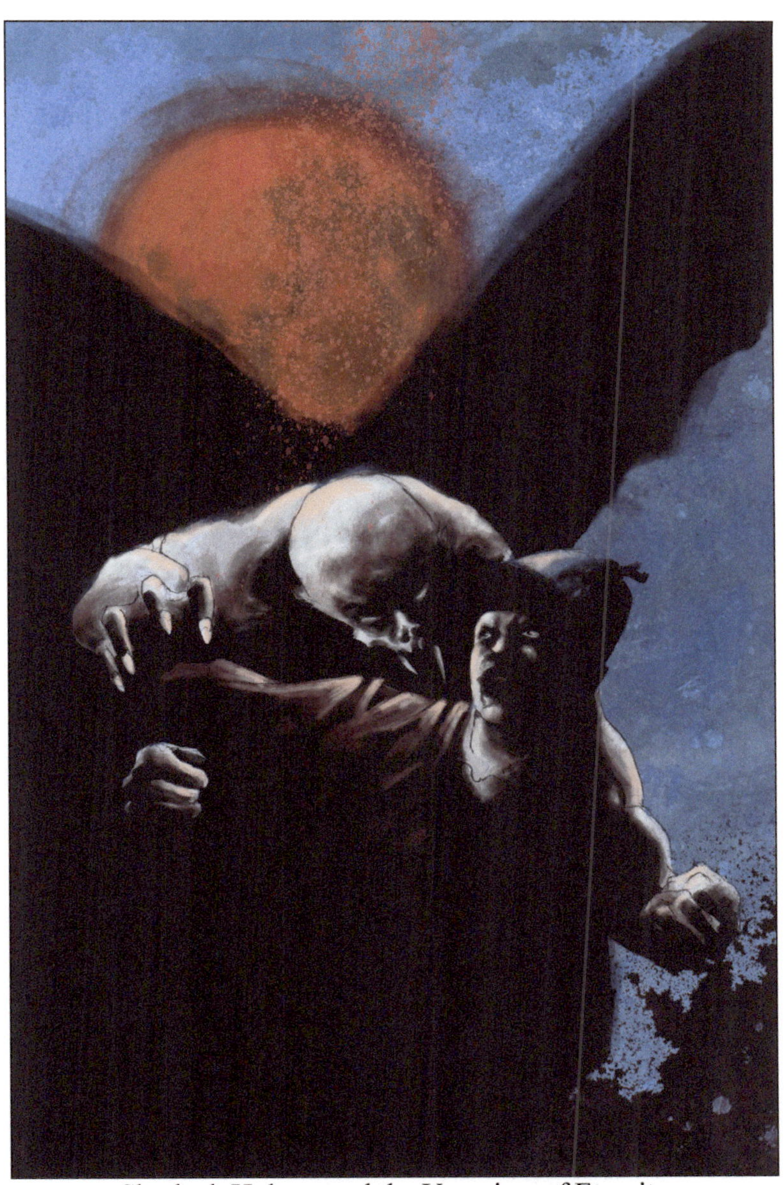

Sherlock Holmes and the Vampires of Eternity

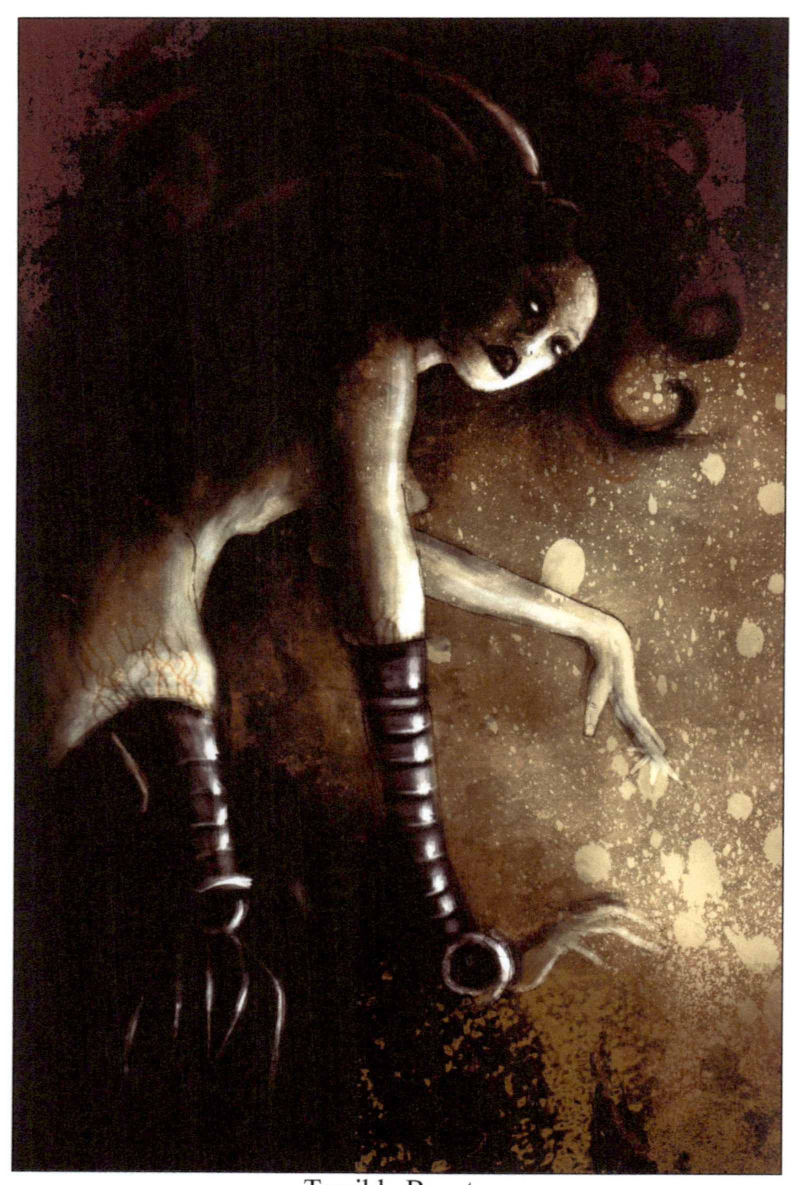

Terrible Beauty

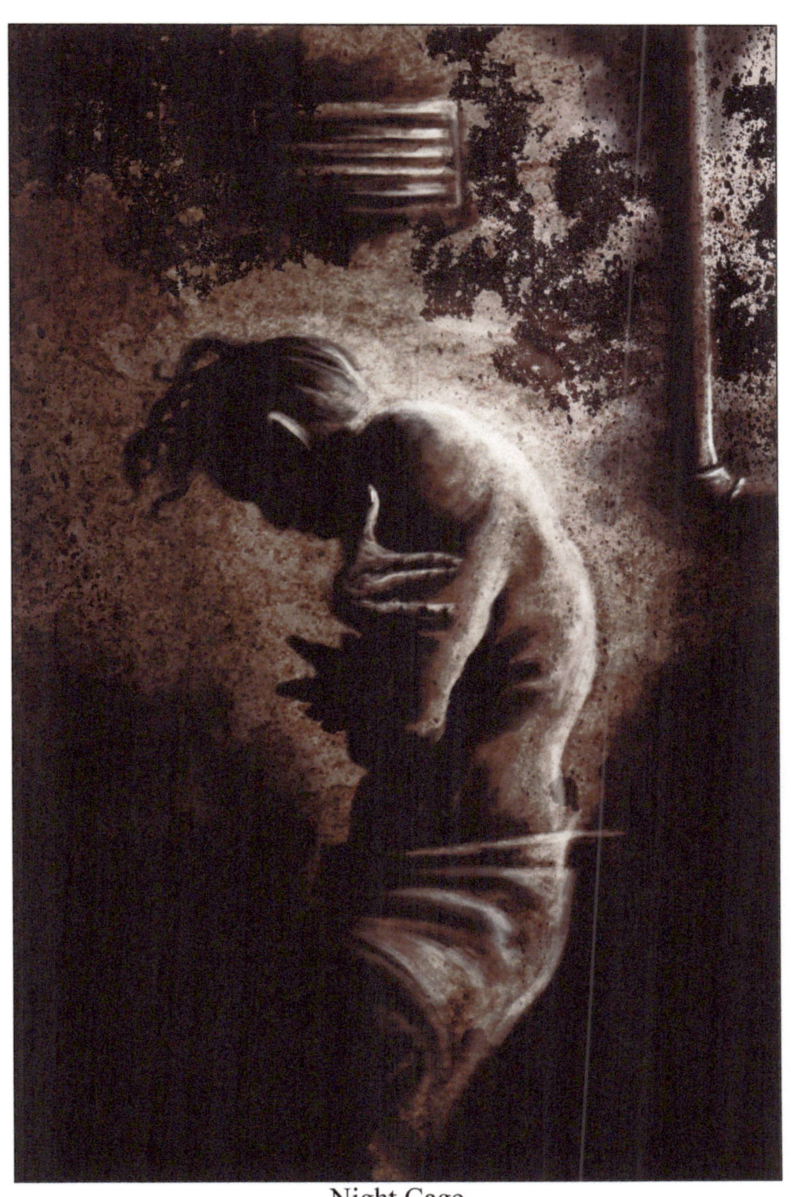

Night Cage

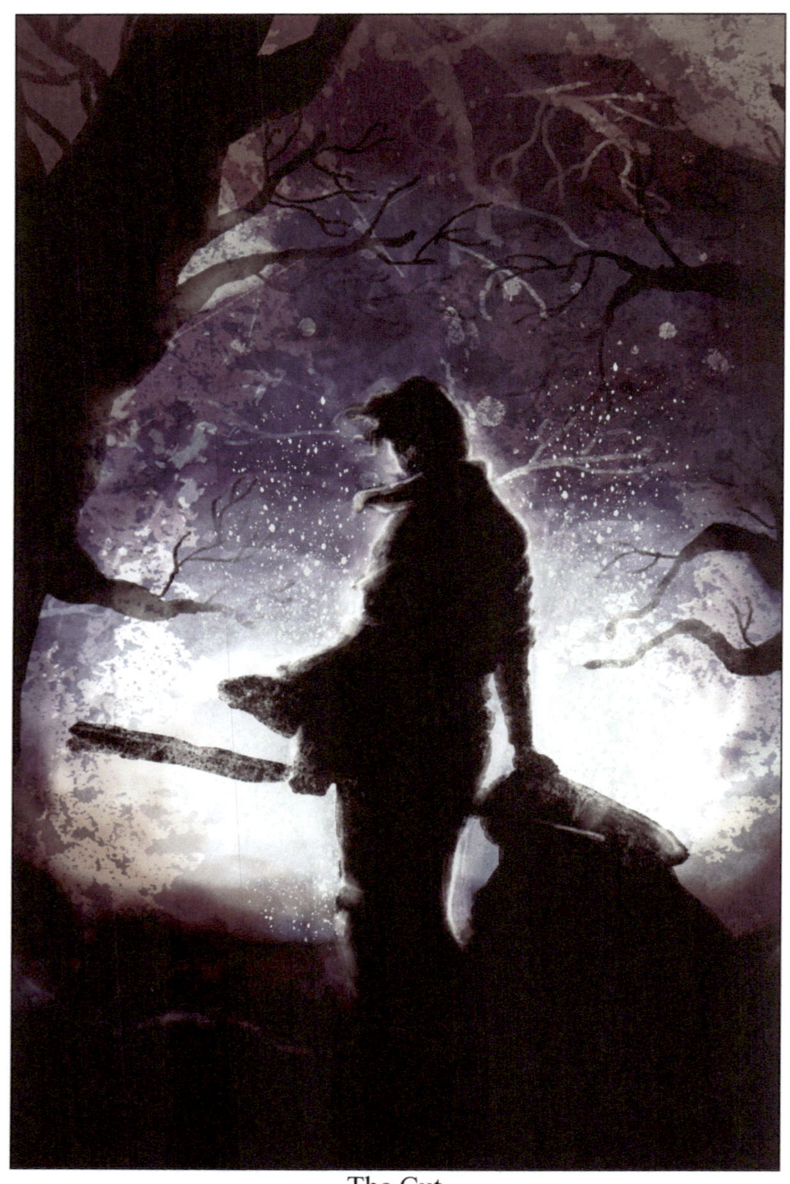

The Cut

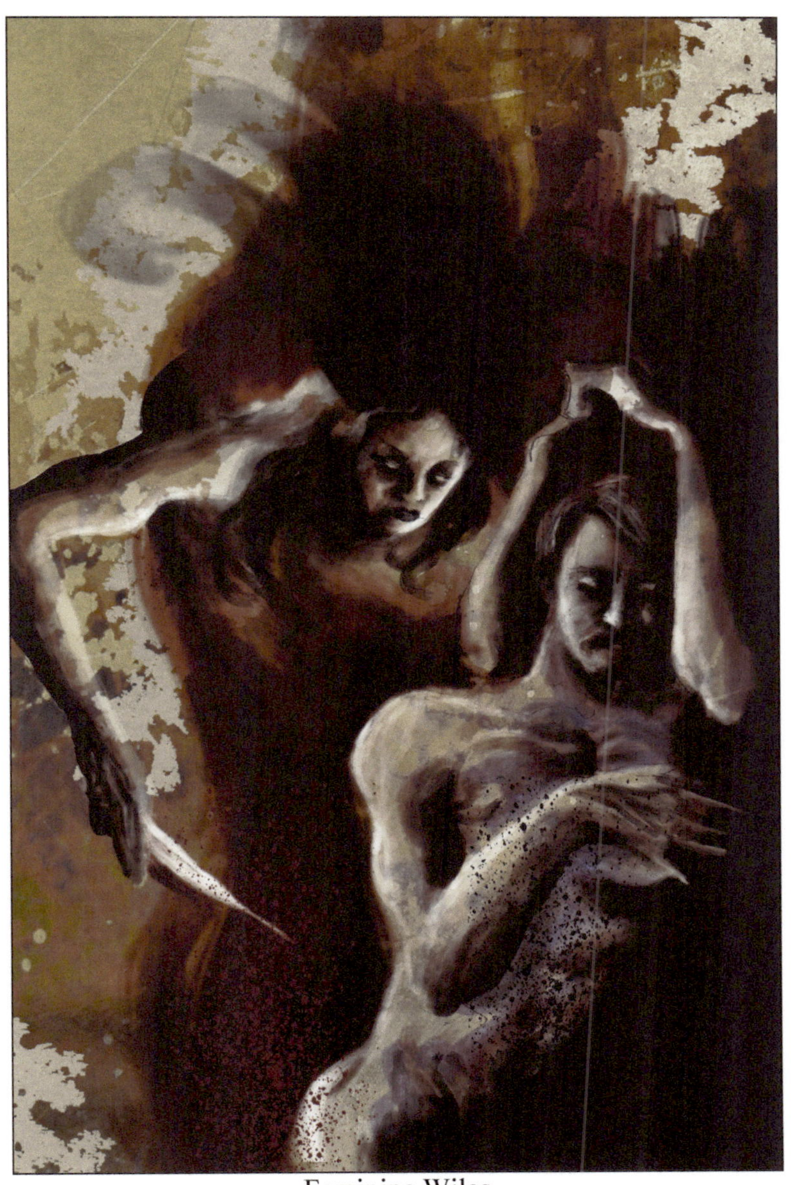

Feminine Wiles

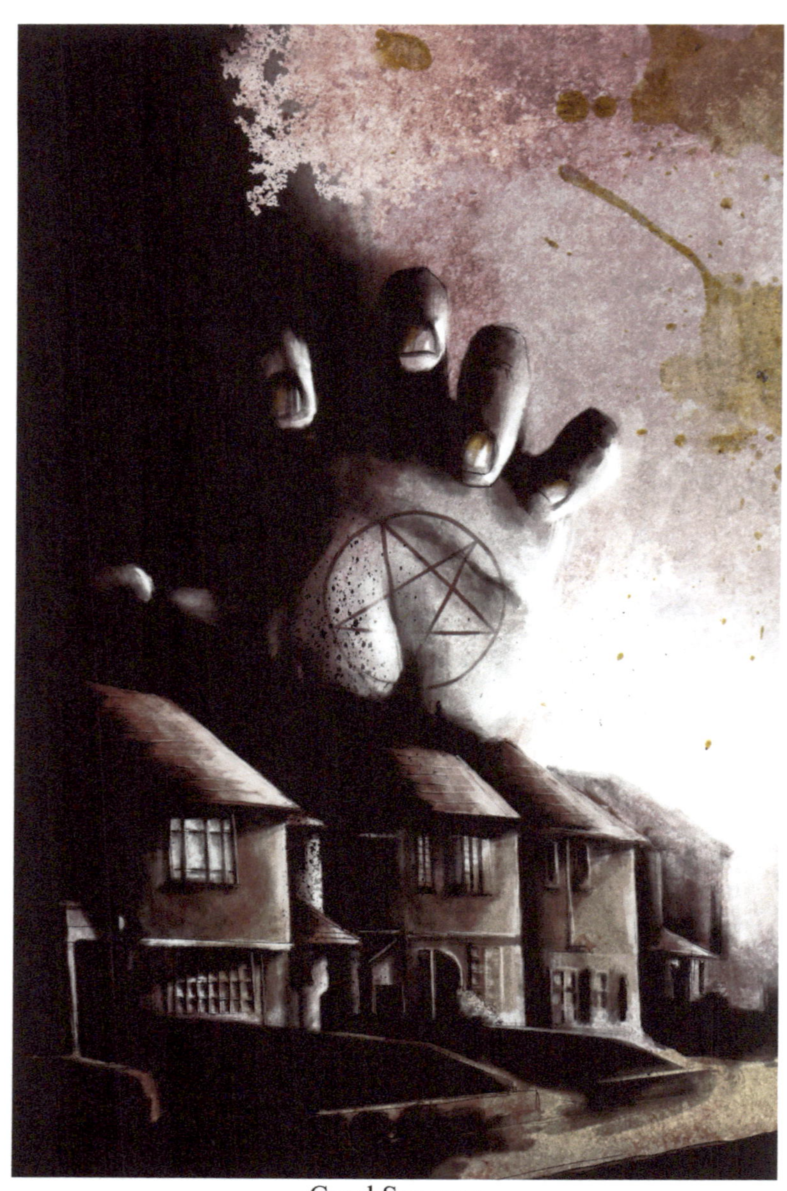

Cruel Summer

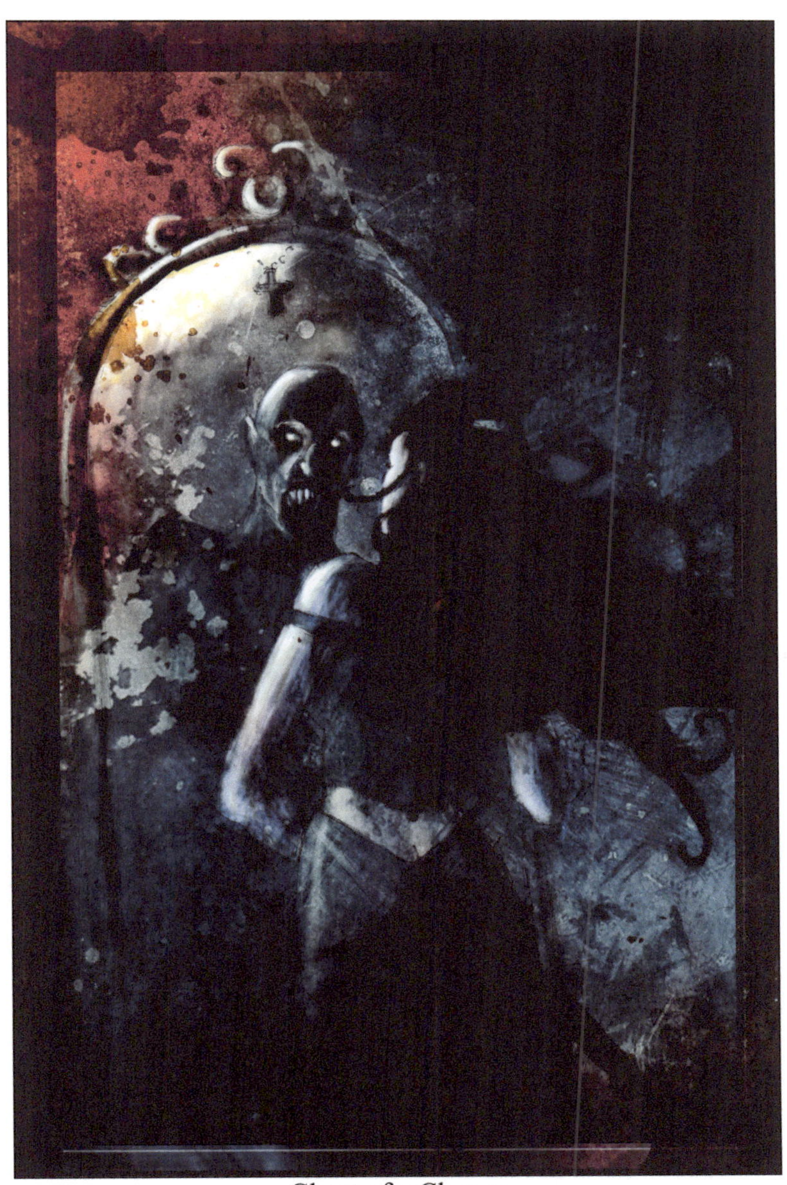

Ghost of a Chance

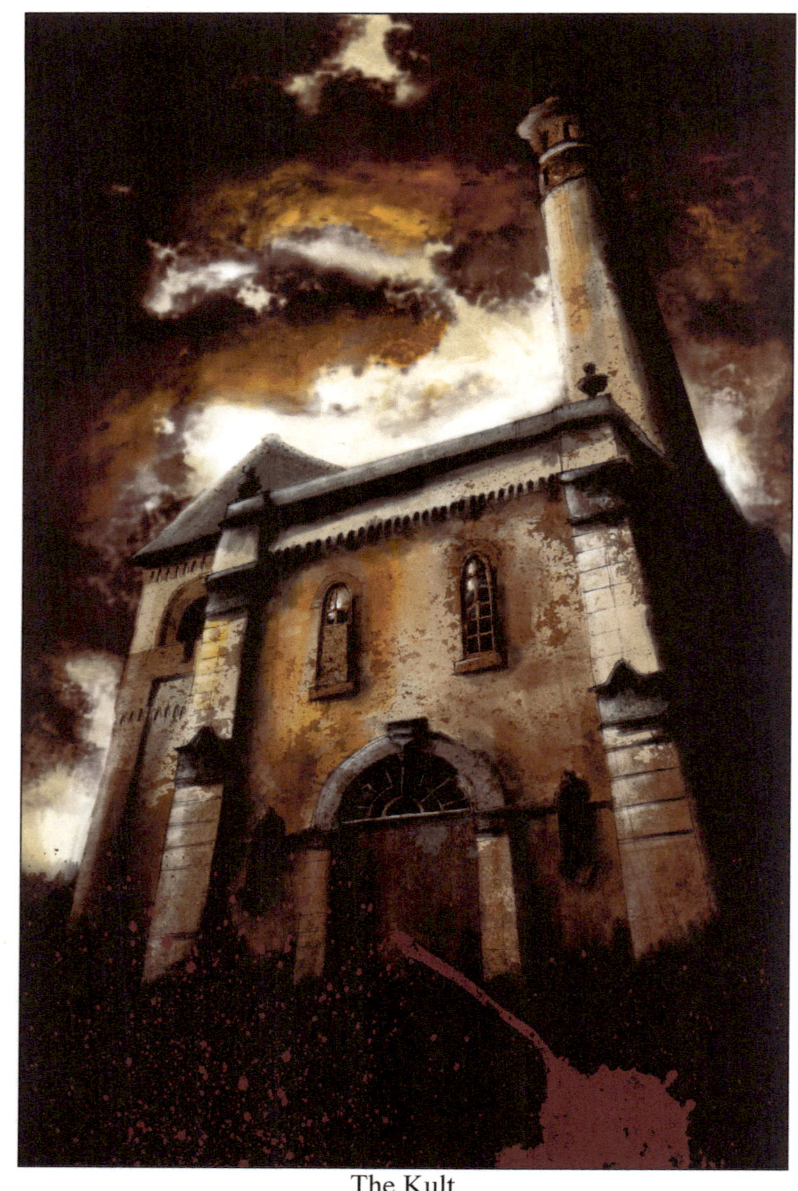

The Kult

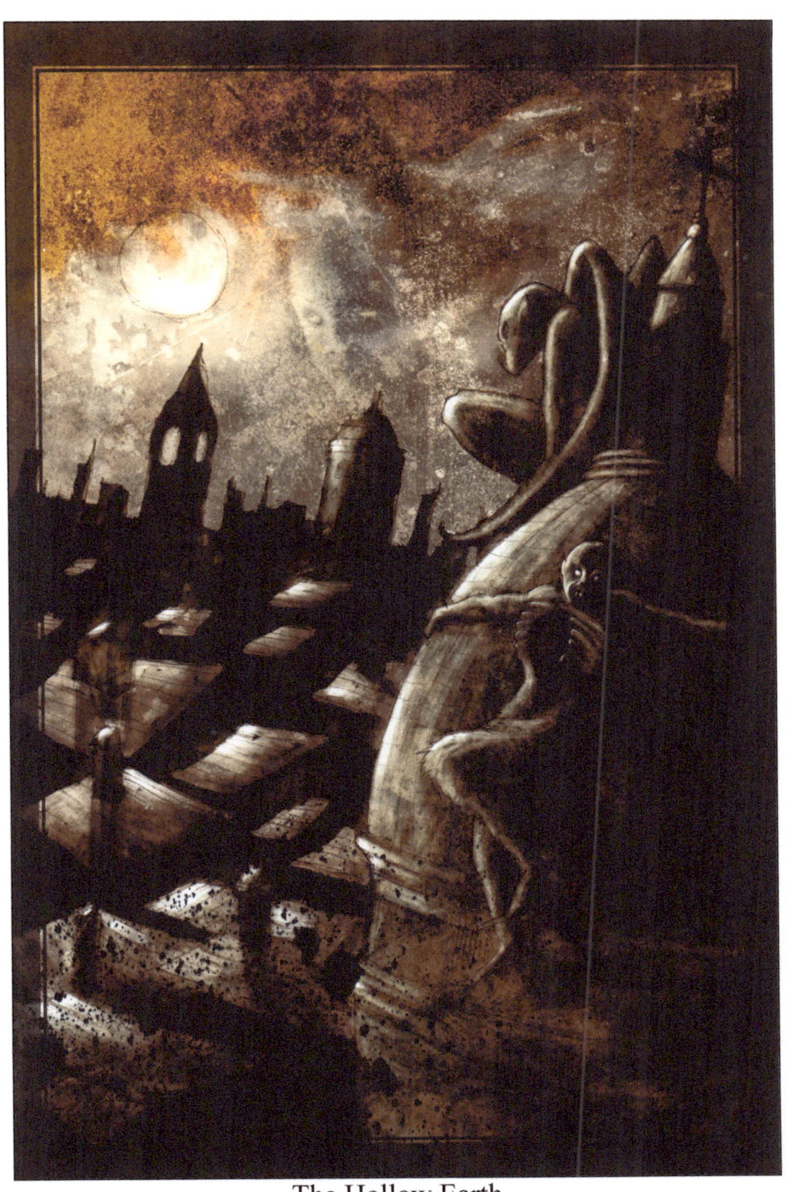

The Hollow Earth

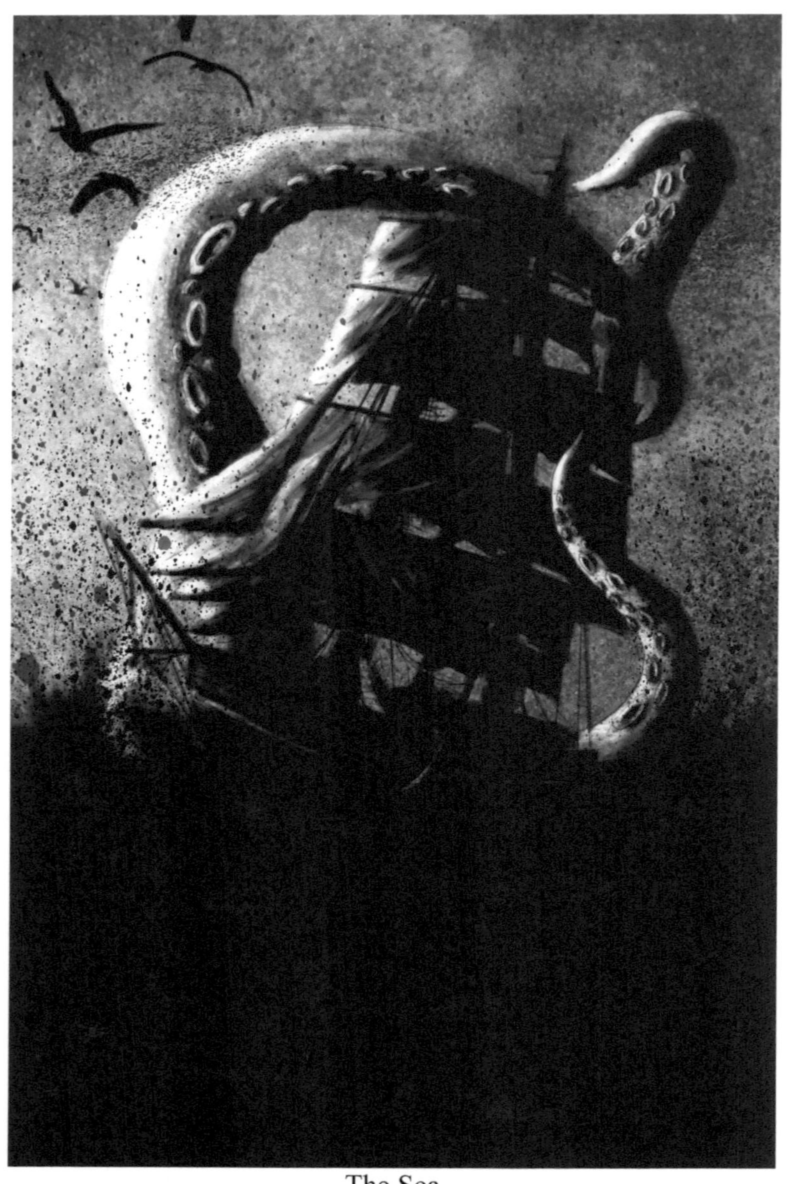

The Sea

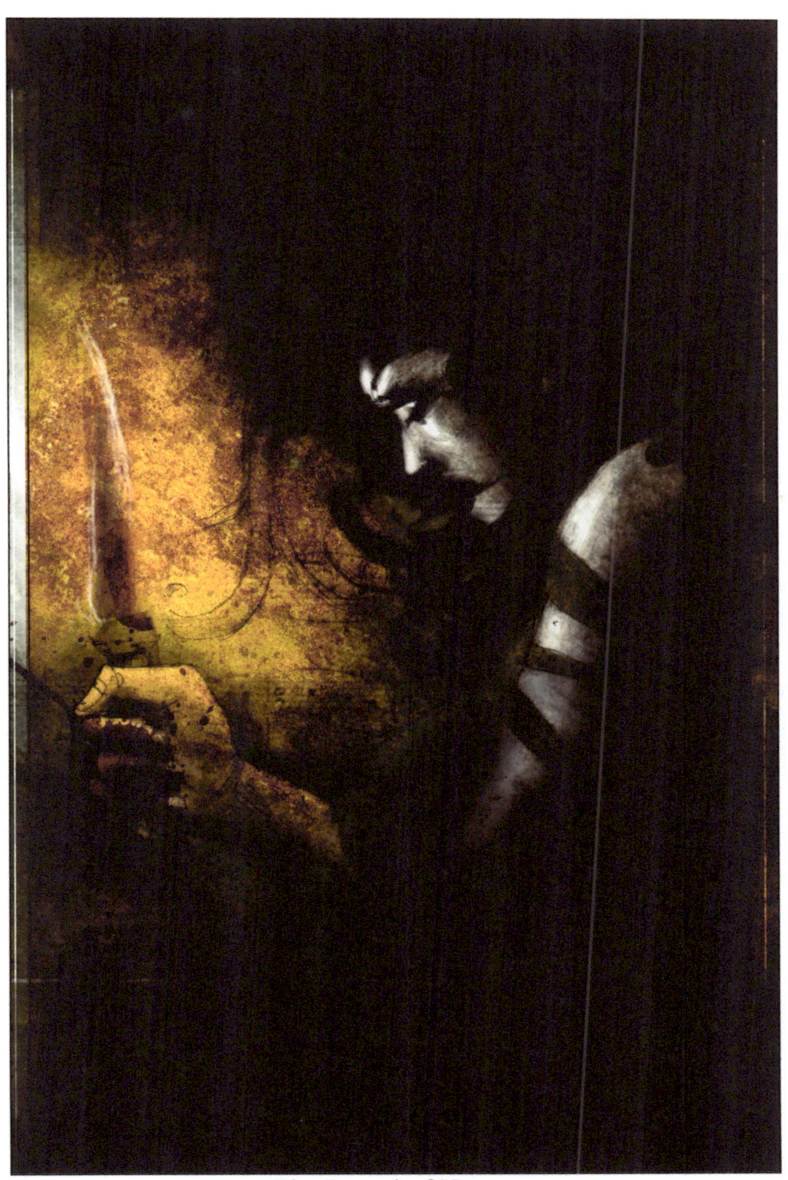

The Sound of Horror

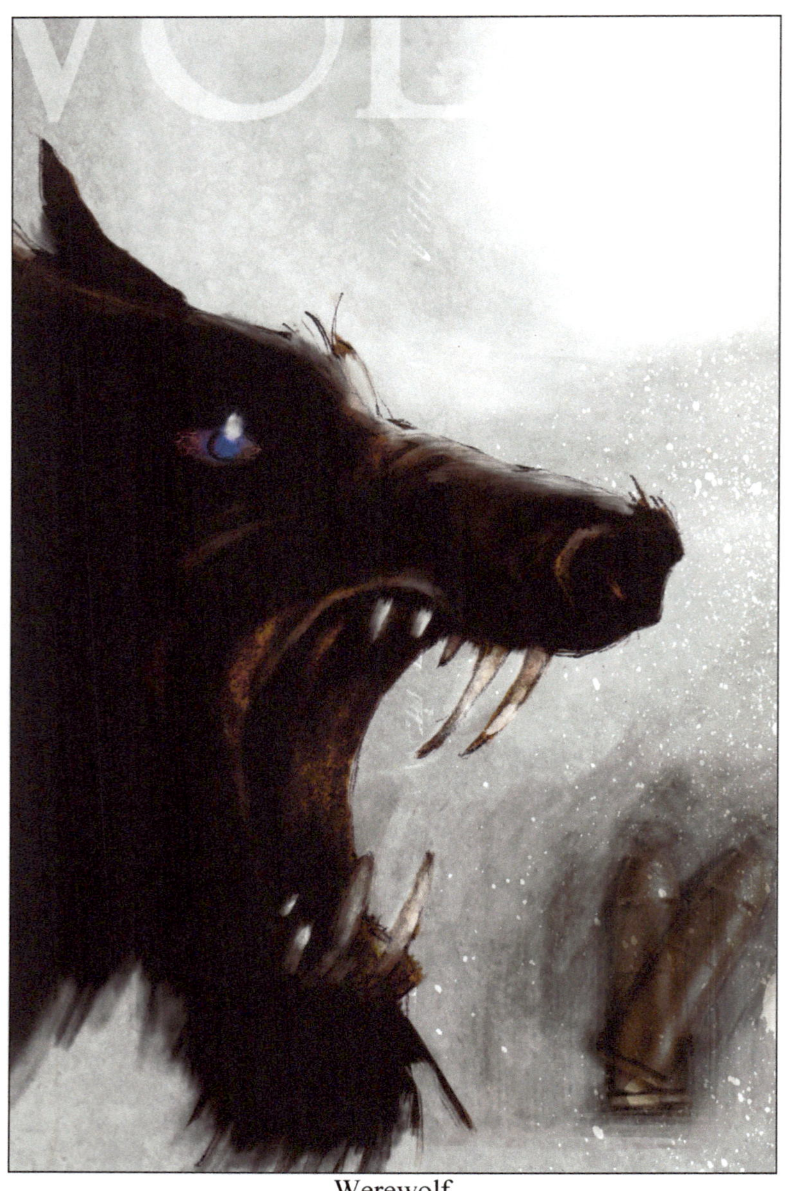

Werewolf

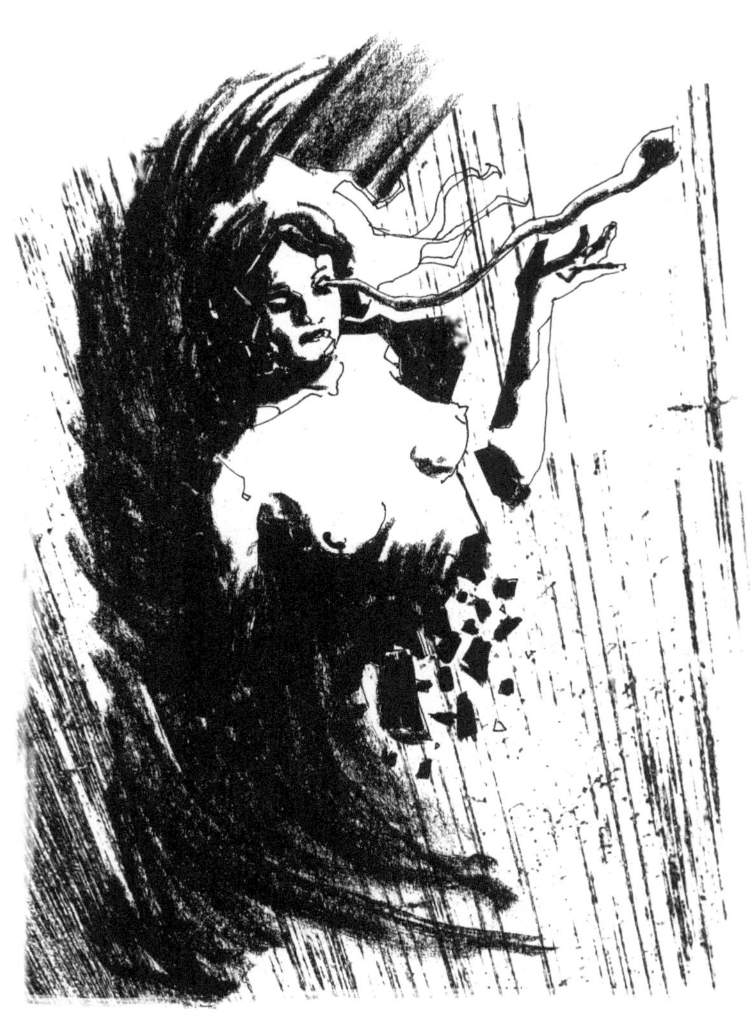

Eye

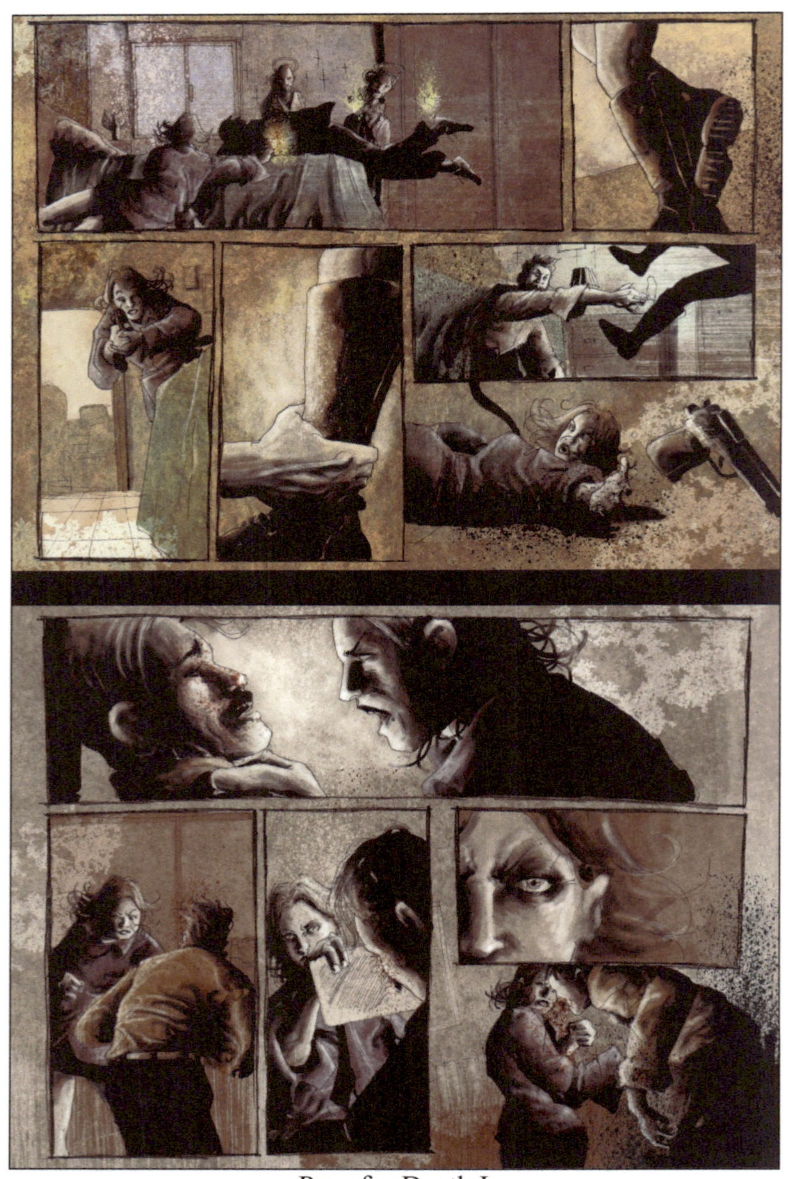

Pray for Death I

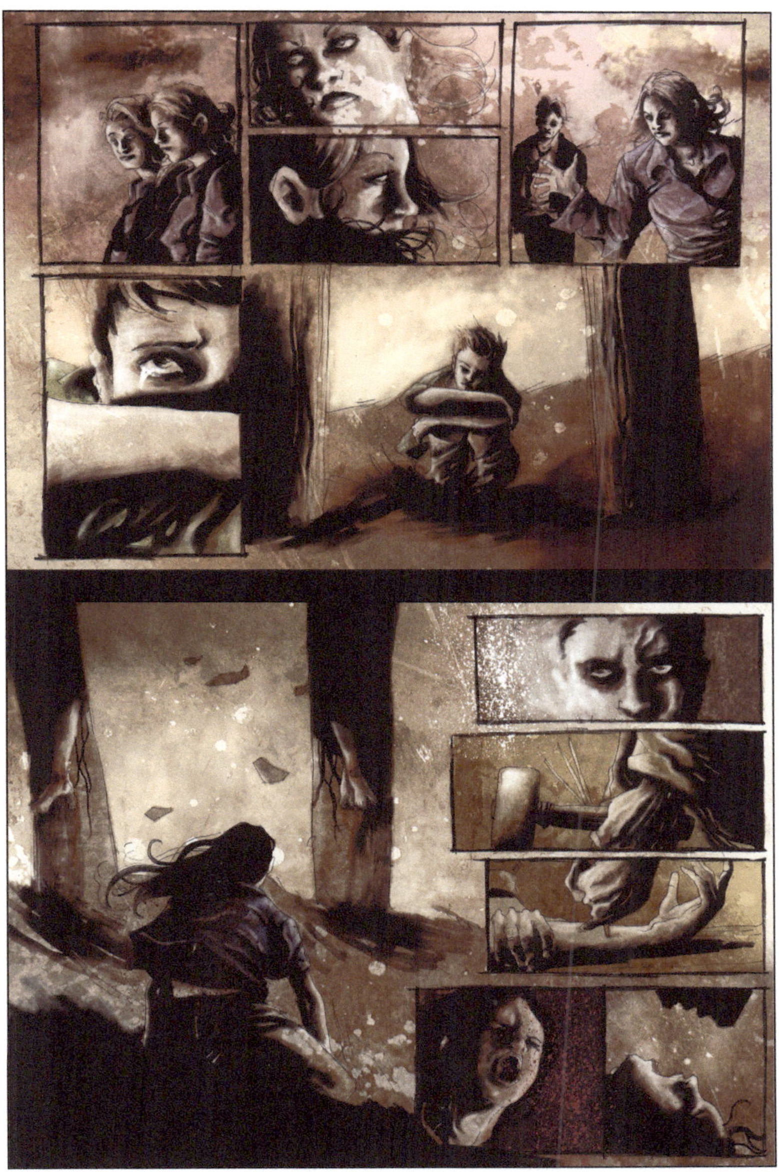

Pray for Death II

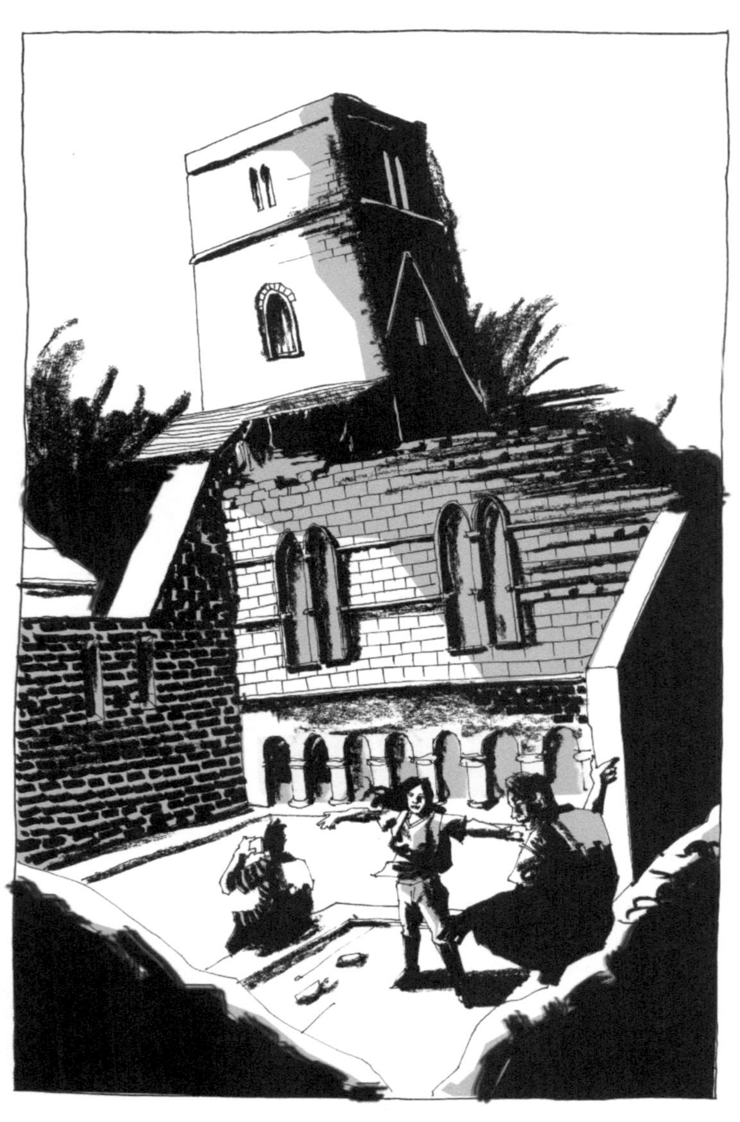

One Last Tear I

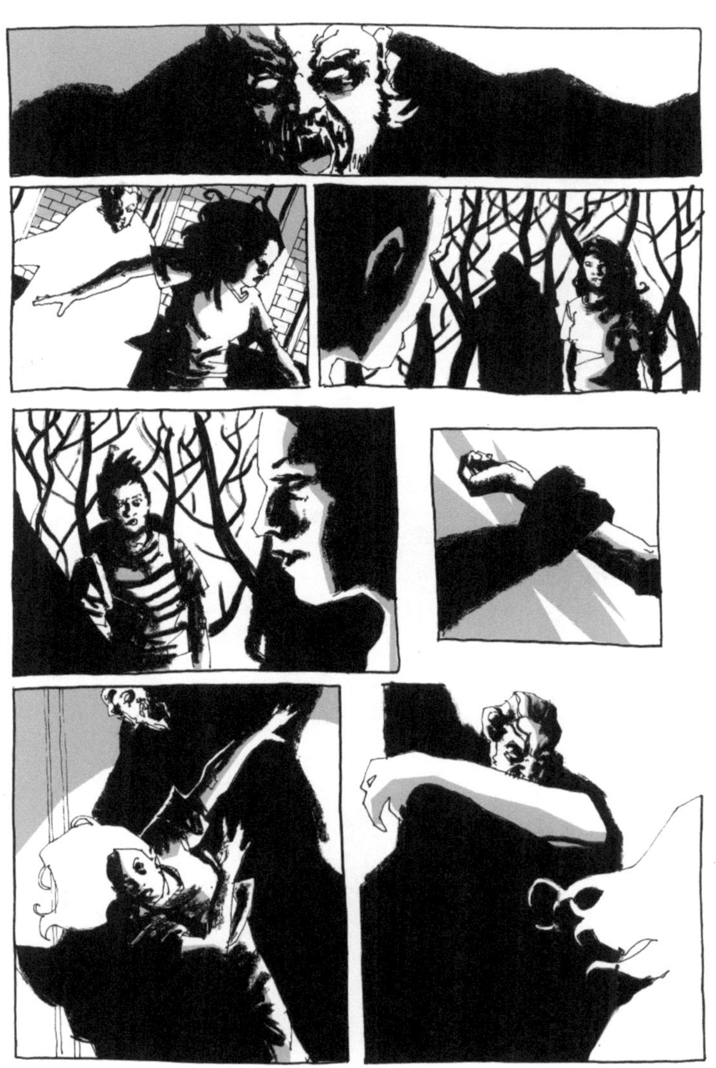

One Last Tear II

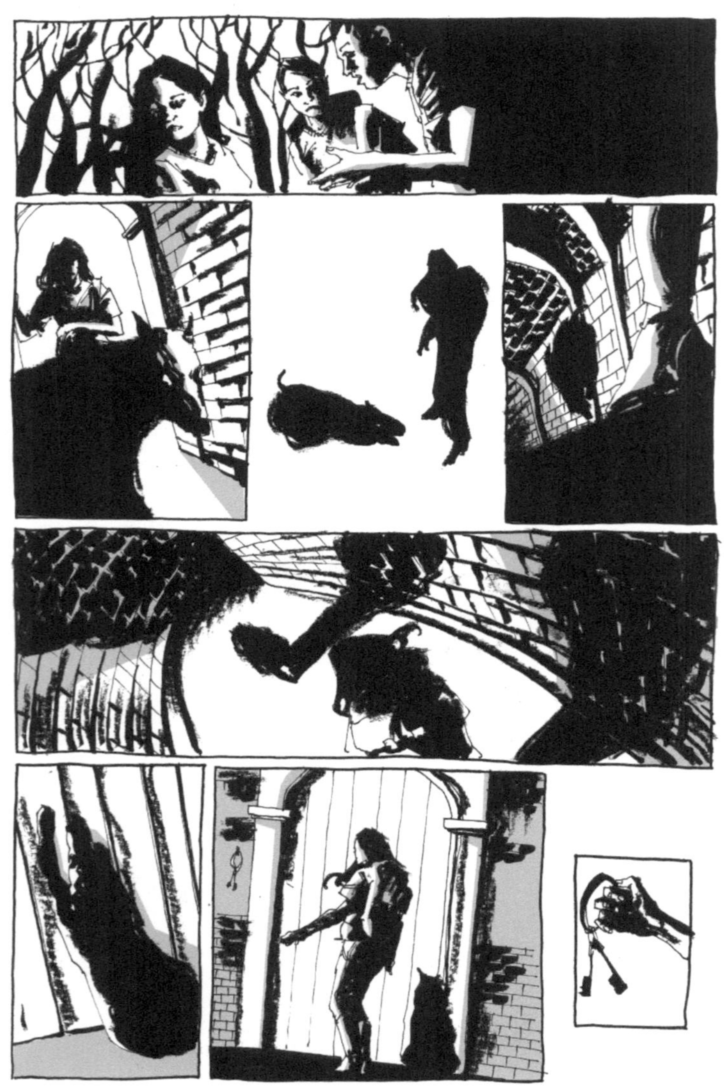

One Last Tear III

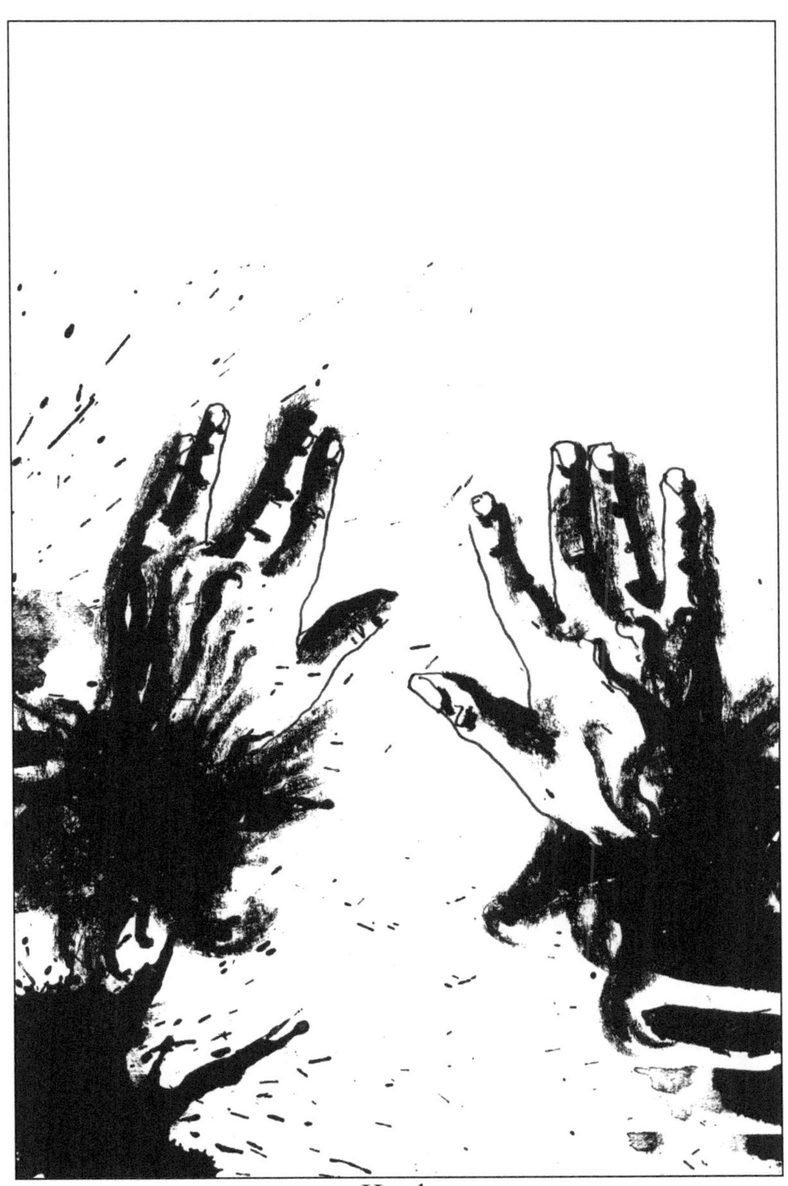

Hands

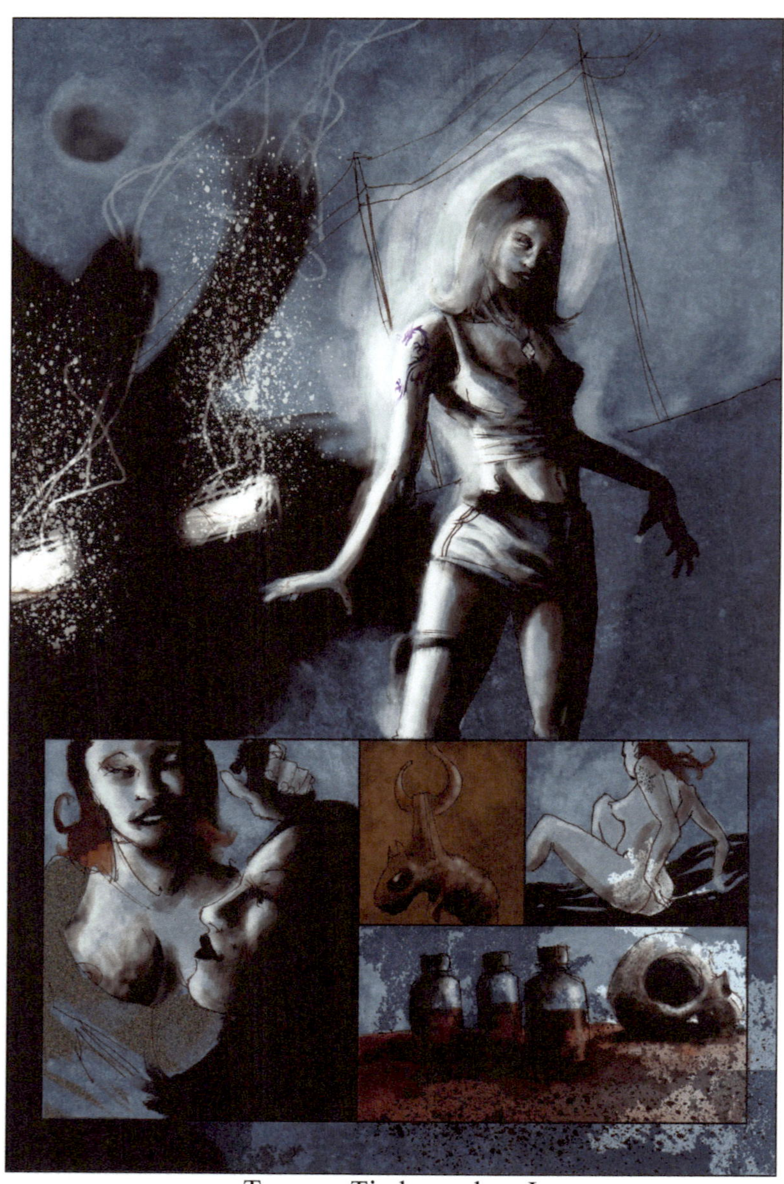

Teenage Timberwolves I

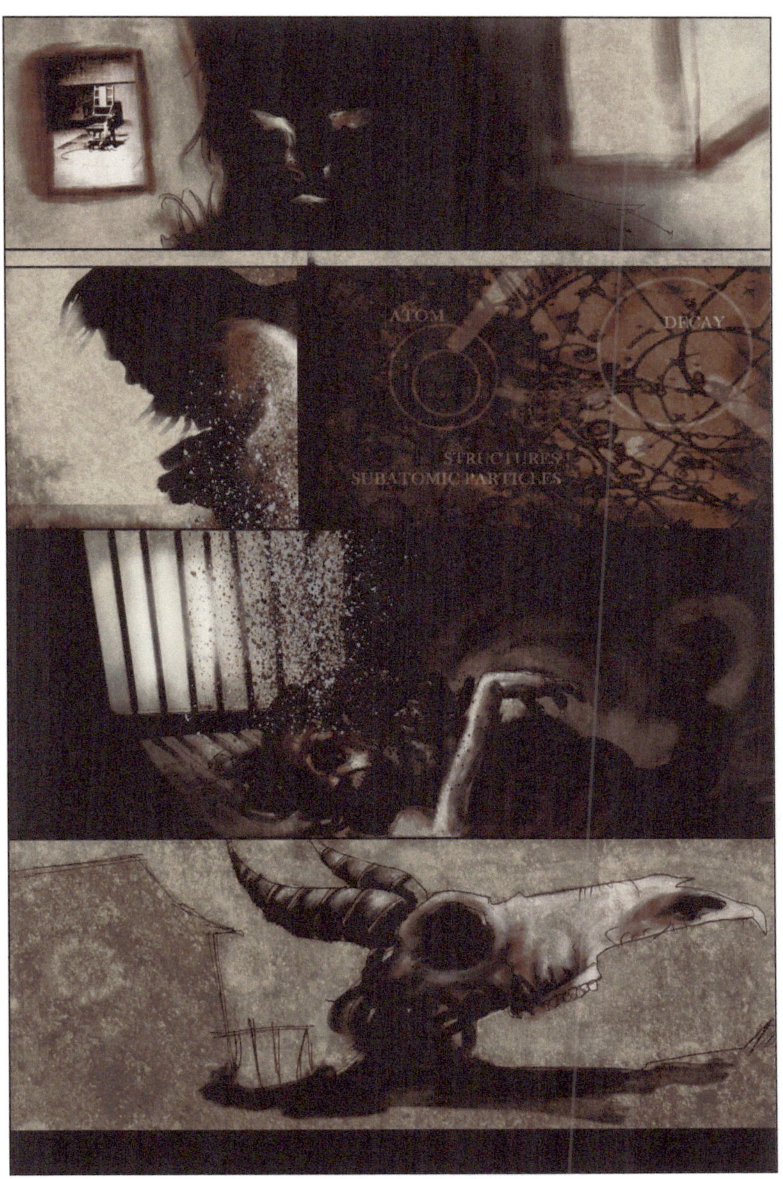

Teenage Timberwolves II

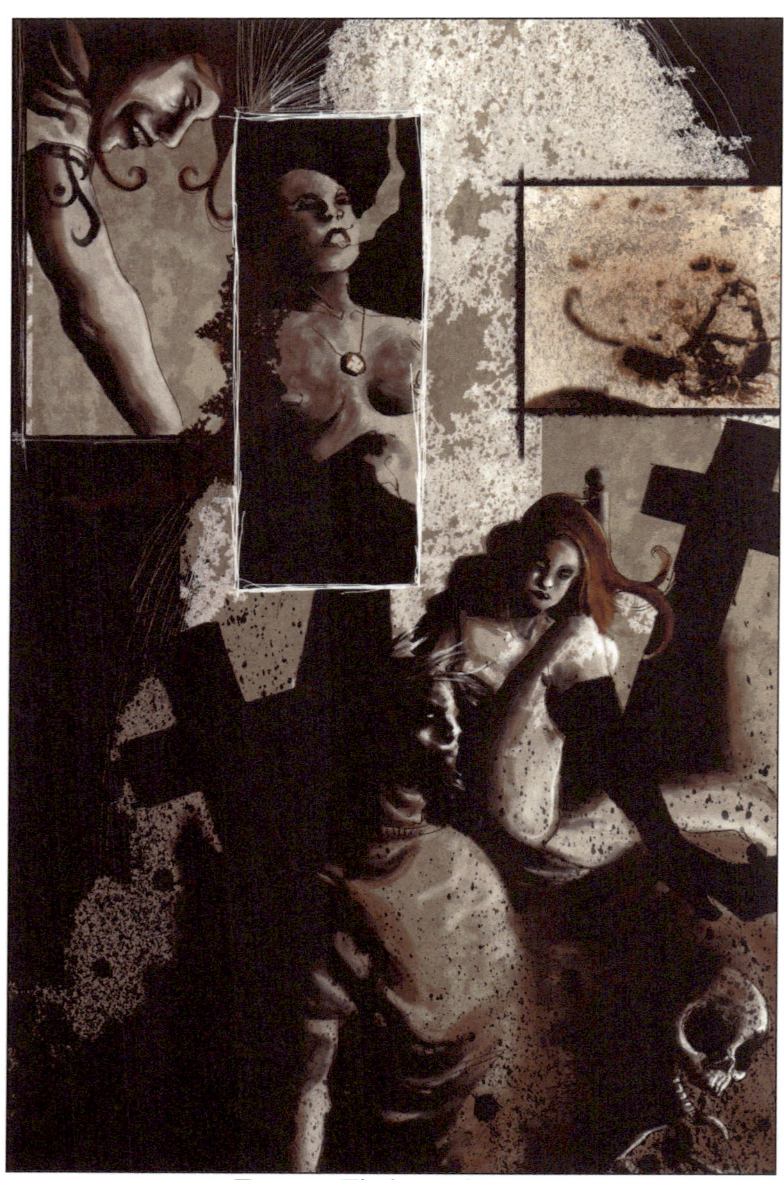

Teenage Timberwolves III

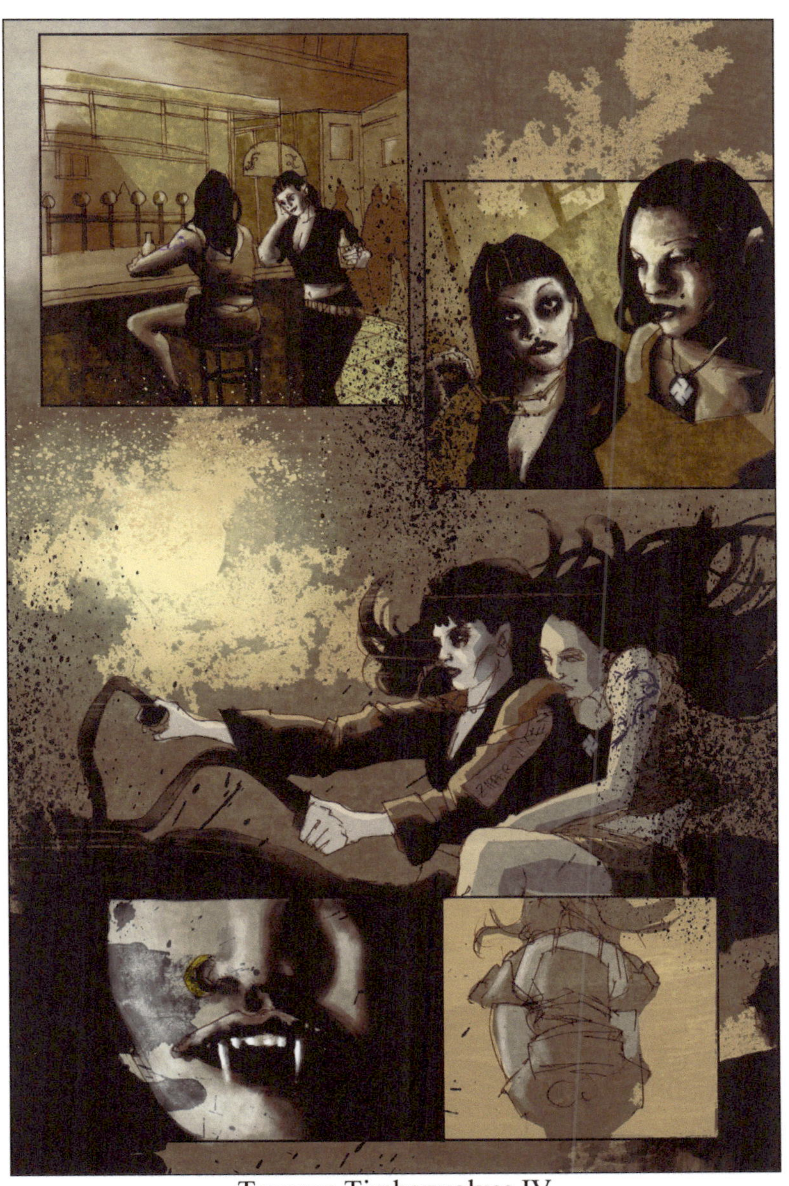

Teenage Timberwolves IV

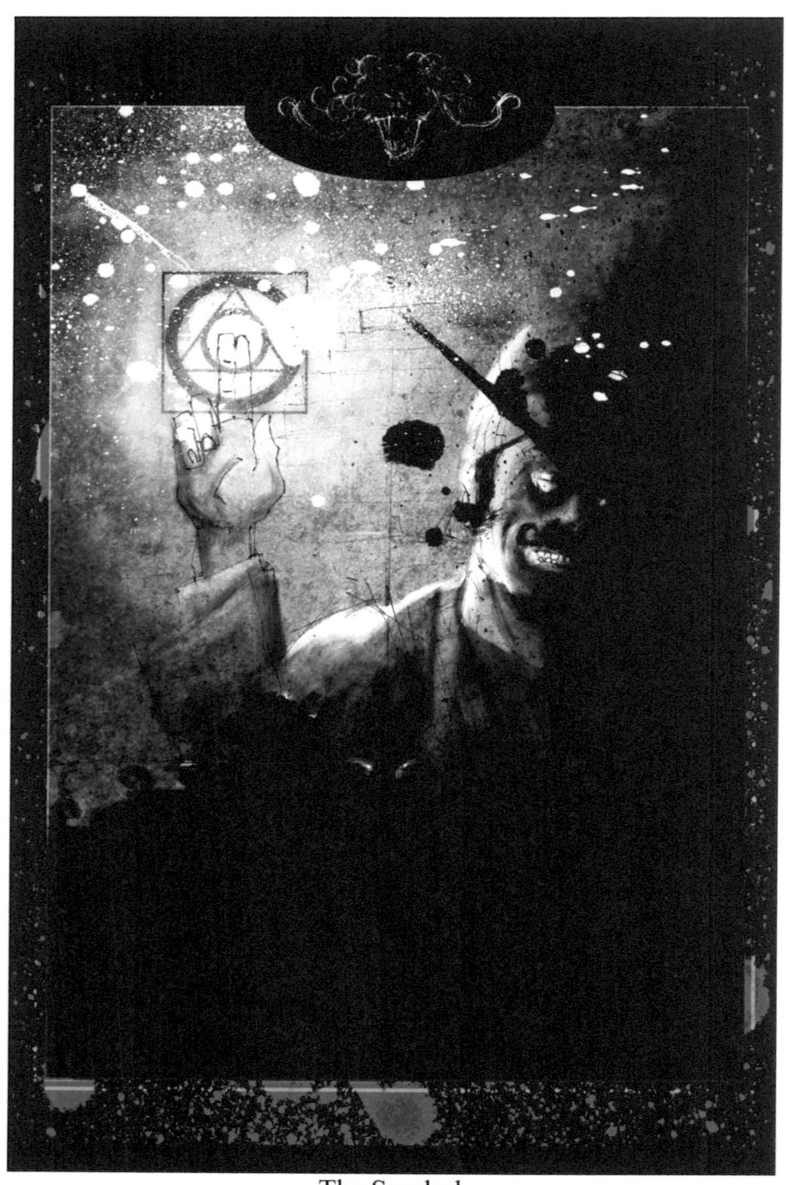

The Symbol

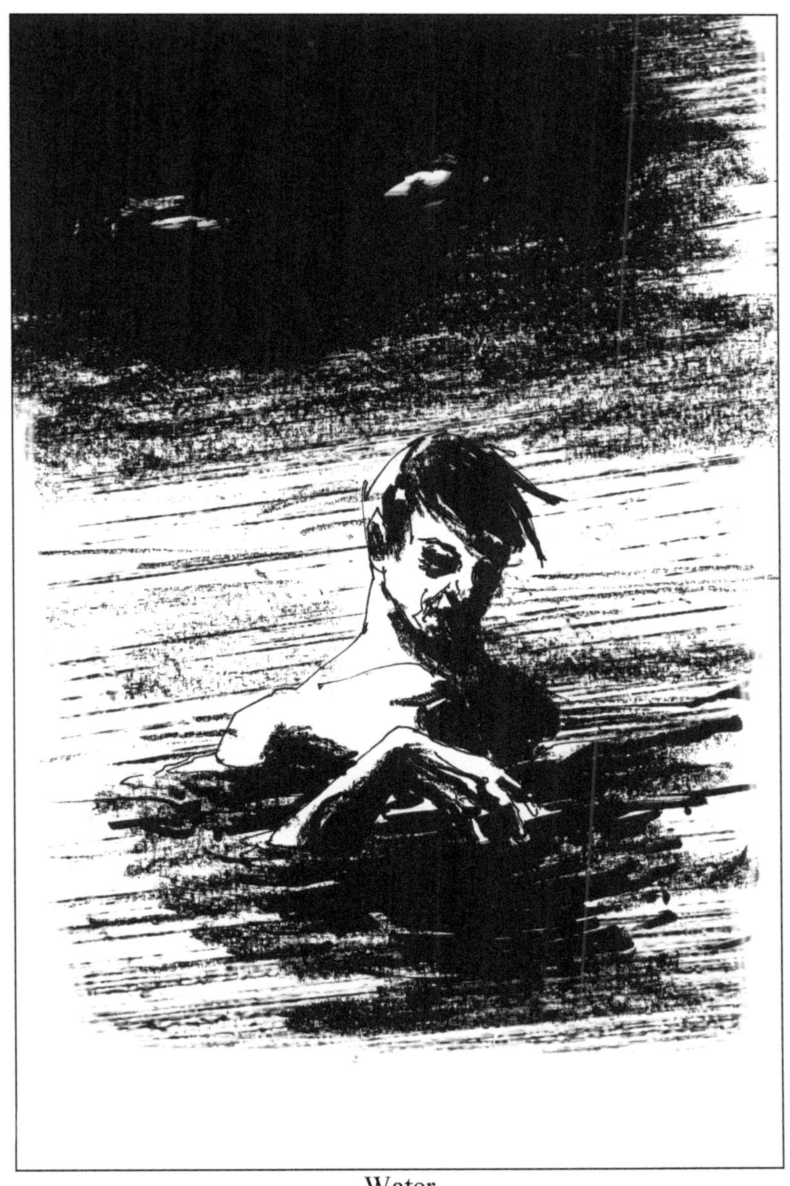

Water

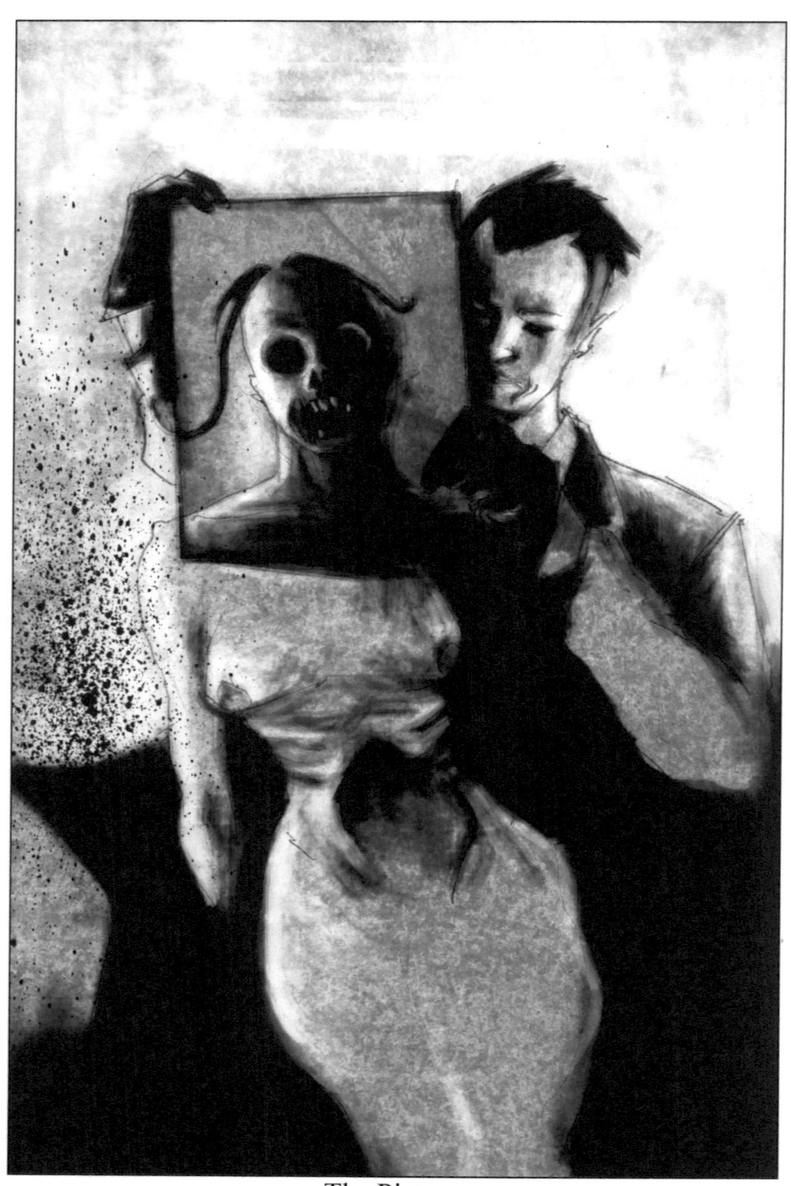

The Picture

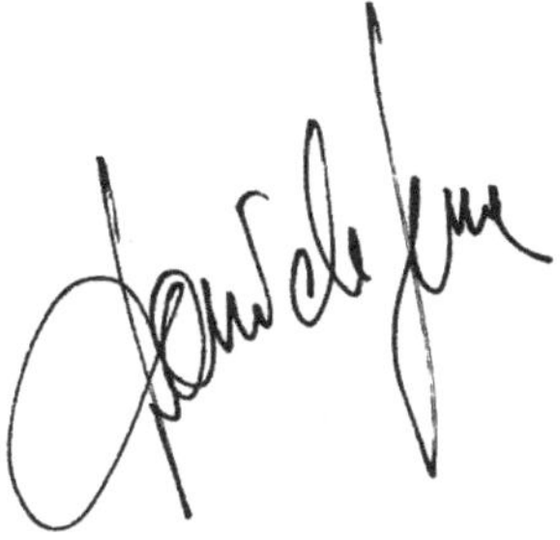

Daniele Serra is a professional illustrator.
His work has been published in Europe, Australia and
the United States, and displayed at various exhibits in Italy.
He has provided illustrations for author such as
Brian Stableford, Rain Graves, Steven Savile, etc.
He has also worked for DC Comics, Cemetery Dance,
Weird Tales magazine and other publications.